THE OLD TESTAMENT
PSEUDEPIGRAPHA

The Old Testament Pseudepigrapha

Patriarchs and Prophets
in Early Judaism

D.S. RUSSELL

FORTRESS PRESS   PHILADELPHIA

Library of Congress Cataloging-in-Publication Data
Russell, D. S. (David Syme), 1916–
Introducing the Old Testament Pseudepigrapha.

Bibliography: p.
Includes indexes.
1. Apocryphal books (Old Testament)—Criticism,
interpretation, etc. I. Title.
BS1700.R87   1988   229'.9106   86–46433
ISBN 0–8006–2055–0

2998C87   Printed in the United Kingdom   1–2055

Contents

Preface

The genesis of this book is to be found in a reading and re-reading of
Stephen's speech in Acts 7 in which he recounts the story of the
patriarchs and other ancient heroes in terms of the coming Christ and
his kingdom. Like the writer of Hebrews 11, with its gallery of saints
who 'all died in faith', his method of interpretation and the use to
which he puts his historical survey are quite different from those of
his Jewish contemporaries. But he is not alone in recalling the merits
of his Hebrew forebears and recounting their exploits and the part
they played in the unfolding purpose of God. These great men of the
past were in fact the subject of many Jewish writings at that time, both
in Palestine itself and also in the Dispersion. This is particularly so of
those books generally called the 'pseudepigrapha' on which I have
chosen to focus attention.

These writings are now much more readily available than they were
only a few years ago. Many of them, however, are not easy to read or
to understand. For this reason I have tried to outline as clearly as
possible the nature of their contents and to pin-point what they have
to say concerning their understanding of the patriarchs and prophets
of old, in whose names most of them were written. It is to be hoped
that this 'introduction' to the Old Testament pseudepigrapha (and to
certain Christian pseudepigrapha reflecting earlier Jewish traditions)
will encourage the reader who wishes to know more, to pursue the
reading and study of these documents still further. They are important,
I believe, in themselves and also for the light they cast on the thinking
of both early Judaism and early church. This book is offered as a 'tool'
which, hopefully, will help to shape the reader's understanding of
both.

I am indebted to many scholars, not least to J. H. Charlesworth for
The Old Testament Pseudepigrapha, edited by him in two volumes.
This publication and that edited by H. F. D. Sparks, *The Apocryphal
Old Testament*, provide invaluable source material.

I am indebted too to Mrs Pat Miles for typing out the manuscript from my inept scrawl, and to my wife for her continuing patience and help.

Bristol, 1986   D. S. RUSSELL

Introduction

The purpose of this volume is to demonstrate from the books generally called 'the pseudepigrapha' the considerable developments that took place in early Judaism relating to the character and function of the patriarchs and prophets in whose names many of them were written. Such developments, of course, were not limited to the pseudepigrapha, and so in chapter 1 a brief outline will be given of similar developments recorded in the Jewish writers Philo and Josephus, in the rabbinic literature and in the Dead Sea scrolls. Nor were they limited to the Jewish literature of that time, for the same process continued in the life of the Christian church which edited, expurgated and interpolated earlier Jewish works and produced pseudepigrapha of its own. Indeed it was within the Christian church that the Jewish pseudepigrapha were preserved and the traditions they contained were treasured. For this reason it is often difficult to know whether a given passage or book is of Jewish or of Christian origin and, if Christian, whether it reflects an earlier Jewish tradition.

A study of the pseudepigrapha involves many problems of a critical nature, introducing questions of text, date, provenance, authorship and the rest. It is not the intention of this book to examine such questions, but rather to build on the findings of scholarship already established and in so doing to point out areas where there is still a lack of scholarly consensus. The aim is, wherever possible, to let these writings speak for themselves, to spell out as clearly as possible their content and meaning and, in particular, to focus attention on the part played by the patriarchs and prophets of Israel as fathers of their people. In this way it is hoped that the reader will gain an insight into the contents and teaching of books which were once popular within both Jewish and Christian traditions, which have survived the centuries in many transcripts and translations (albeit in not a few cases in obscurity) and deserve to be better known by reason of their historical and religious contribution to our understanding of early Judaism and the early church.

This is not the place to attempt an evaluation of the worth of these writings in respect of the contribution they make to our understanding of the historical, cultural, social and religious life of early Judaism. Suffice to say that they should not be lightly dismissed as either fabrications or the work of over-heated imaginations or the garbled record of wild speculations. On the contrary, these writings are the work of men of faith who saw penetratingly beyond the seen to the unseen and for whom 'the other world' of the spirit impinged on the life of 'this world' in such a way that they could hardly at times distinguish the one from the other. The discerning reader will be able to sift the gold from the dross and find enrichment in their pages.

But what are these 'pseudepigrapha'? This Greek word, meaning 'with false subscription' and so 'books written under an assumed name', is notoriously difficult to define. If the truth be told, it is at best an inappropriate word if only because some of the books normally listed as such are not themselves pseudepigraphical, whilst there are others not included which obviously are! It is adopted here, however, simply because it is the word in general use and is recognized internationally.

The English-speaking reader will be rather puzzled to find quite different lists of such books in three collections of pseudepigrapha at his disposal. The first of these was published many years ago under the editorship of R. H. Charles (*The Apocrypha and Pseudepigrapha of the Old Testament*, vol. 2, 1913) and contained the text of seventeen writings. The second was edited many years later by H. F. D. Sparks (*The Apocryphal Old Testament*, 1983) who omitted seven of those included by Charles and added another fifteen, making twenty-five altogether. The third was edited by J. H. Charlesworth (*The Old Testament Pseudepigrapha*, vols. 1 and 2, 1984 and 1985) which produced the text of no fewer than fifty-two pseudepigraphical books together with a supplement containing portions of another thirteen. The reason for this considerable diversity is to be found in the fact that there has been no agreement concerning the actual criteria by which the books in such a list are to be judged.

Generally speaking, the expression 'pseudepigrapha', in its early Jewish context, may be said to refer to a body of diverse writings in the Jewish or Jewish-Christian traditions which (a) are not included in the Old or New Testaments, the Apocrypha and the rabbinic literature, (b) are associated with the biblical books or biblical characters, (c) are more often than not written in the name of some ancient biblical worthy, (d) convey a message from God that is relevant to the time at which the books were written and (e) are written during the period 200 BC – AD 200 or, if later than this, preserve Jewish traditions of that same period.

For the purpose of such a definition the 'Apocrypha' should be regarded as comprising those 'extra-canonical' books to be found in most (Greek) Septuagint manuscripts but not those in the (Latin) Vulgate. This would mean including the Psalms of Solomon, the Prayer of Manasseh. IV Ezra (= II Esdras), III and IV Maccabees and Psalm 151 within the 'Pseudepigrapha' and not within the 'Apocrypha'. Apart from commentaries and other works peculiar to the Covenanters of Qumran, there are other writings and fragments of writings among the Dead Sea scrolls which have much in common with certain of the known pseudepigrapha, writings such as the Genesis Apocryphon, the Temple Scroll and the Book of Mysteries. Whether or not these are to be included in the list of pseudepigrapha is a moot point; in any case, both should be read together to gain a clearer picture of those 'intertestamental' years. In this present volume the Book of Daniel has been included for examination even though it comes within the Old Testament canon, since its appearance around the year 165/4 BC falls within the period under discussion and because it has something in common with other non-canonical apocalyptic writings among the pseudepigrapha which may reflect an ongoing 'Daniel tradition'.

In the following chapters quotations from the pseudepigrapha will be taken, for the most part, from J. H. Charlesworth's *The Old Testament Pseudepigrapha*, as will also the dates of writing suggested there. His two volumes have made available many pseudepigraphical writings hitherto unknown to the general reader or else not readily accessible. Some of these are not apposite to the subject of this present book and so receive no mention in the following pages – writings such as Ahiqar (seventh to sixth century BC), the Letter of Aristeas (third century BC to first century AD), Psalms of Solomon (first century BC) and Odes of Solomon (late first to early second century AD). Most of the others, however, do relate to either the patriarchs or the prophets and are examined accordingly. A 'check-list' of these, set out in chronological order, may be found helpful for reference:

Artapanus (third to second century BC)
Aristobulus (second century BC)

Greek Apocalypse of Ezra (second to ninth century AD)
History of Joseph (before fourth century AD)
Vision of Ezra (fourth to seventh century AD)
Questions of Ezra (date unknown)
III (Hebrew Apocalypse of) Enoch (fifth to sixth century AD)
Revelation of Ezra (before ninth century AD)

I

Ancient Heroes

1. The patriarchs: an idealized picture

The God of Israel is the God of Abraham, Isaac and Jacob. They, together with all the other patriarchs, held a place of high honour in the history of 'God's chosen people'. The place they held among the Jews at the beginning of the so-called intertestamental period is well expressed by Ben Sira the scribe, writing about 180 BC, in his great hymn 'in praise of famous men':

> Abraham was the great father of a multitude of nations,
> and no one has been found like him in glory;
> He kept the law of the Most High,
> and was taken into covenant with him . . .
> Moses whose memory is blessed,
> (God) made him equal in glory to the holy ones . . .
> No one like Enoch has been created on earth,
> for he was taken up from the earth.
> And no man like Joseph has been born,
> and his bones are cared for.
> Shem and Seth were honoured among men,
> and Adam among every living being in creation (Ecclus. 44.19f.;
> 45.1f.; 49.14ff.).

In the years that followed Ben Sira and on into the Christian era the patriarchs gained a new prominence and popularity within Judaism. The stories told of them in scripture came to be embellished or amplified or altered in such a way as to enhance their reputation out of all recognition. Legends grew up around them, miracles were

1

attributed to them and rewards were given by a grateful God by reason of the merit they displayed.

Indeed, such was their goodness, their wisdom and their ability that they assumed at times superhuman qualities. In this connection J. D. G. Dunn describes as 'striking' 'the degree to which, despite its monotheism, Judaism in the first century AD and thereafter could accommodate talk of some of its great figures of the past in terms approaching deity' (*Christology in the Making*, 1980, p. 17). Thus it is suggested that Jacob was really the incarnation of an archangel (The Prayer of Joseph 3, Frag. A), that Enoch, who 'walked with God and was not', went on his departure to the Garden of Eden (Jub. 4.21) or to heaven itself (I En. 12.4) where he appeared as the heavenly Son of Man (I En. 71.14) or as the archangel Metatron (III En. 3.16); that Abel (Test. of Abr. 13.2f.) and Melchizedek (11 Q Melch., a fragment among the Dead Sea scrolls) were apparently presented as heavenly judges seated, like Moses, on thrones of glory, exercising judgment over the destinies of men; and that Moses was likewise offered a heavenly throne (Ezekiel the Tragedian ll.73ff.) and vested with divine qualities (Cf. Philo, Josephus and the Assumption of Moses).

'What has emerged', writes Christopher Rowland, 'is a complex pattern of ideas concerning the heavenly position of righteous men . . . For the Jew to have called another being "God" or to have supposed that divine characteristics may have been showed by an exalted man of old seems to have been part of an accepted part of Jewish thought among some of the groups during this period' (*Christian Origins*, 1985, p. 38).

(a) In Philo

The status now accorded to the patriarchs is well illustrated in the writings of the Jewish philosopher Philo (20 BC – AD 50), a contemporary of Jesus, in his treatises 'On Abraham', 'On Isaac' (now lost), 'On Jacob' (now lost) and 'On Joseph' and more especially in his more extensive 'Life of Moses'. These works illustrate well not simply that these men were highly honoured, but also that they were idealized beyond anything to be found in the scriptural record.

In the case of Philo this was often done by making use of allegory and by equating the names of the patriarchs with those virtues so highly prized by the Greek world of that time. The very title of his treatise on Abraham is itself an indication of this. It reads, 'The Life of a Wise Man made Perfect by Instruction, or on the Unwritten Law, that is to say, on Abraham'. According to Philo, the Logos, as an expression of divine reason and divine law, found personal expression in men like Enoch, Noah, Abraham, Isaac and Jacob and supremely in Moses the great lawgiver who was able to penetrate the hidden secrets of God. But even before the law had been revealed to Moses on Sinai, the patriarchs had been aware of it and had lived by it. Abraham can thus be described as 'the unwritten law and justice', a supremely wise man in whom the most coveted virtues reside. Through him men may enter into an understanding of the law of God in its most manifest form.

But Moses, the one to whom that law had been revealed at Sinai, was the man in whom the virtues found their supreme expression, the ideal man, the very embodiment and expression of philosophy and learning. At the feet of wise men of many nations he had learned astronomy, literature, mathematics and philosphy. He was expert in the arts and the sciences, in music and in mystical signs. So brilliant a genius was he that he speedily outstripped his teachers in knowledge and wisdom. God recognized the excellence not only of his piety, but also of his achievements and gave him a place of supreme authority 'as a well deserved reward'.

(b) In Josephus

The Jewish historian Josephus (AD 37–100), who acknowledges his indebtedness for much of his material to earlier writers, is equally fulsome in his praise. He describes Abraham, for example, as 'a man of ready intelligence on all matters' with 'loftier conceptions of virtue than the rest of mankind' and skilled in 'celestial phenomena' (*Ant.* I.155). He is 'a man of extreme sagacity . . . gifted with high intelligence' who ' introduced the Egyptians to arithmetic and transmitted to them the laws of astronomy' (*Ant.* I.161–168), 'a man in every virtue supreme who received from God the due meed of honour for his zeal in his service' (*Ant.* I.256).

The same high praise is heaped on Moses who 'gave signal proof of his merits' (*Ant.* II.238), his sagacity (*Ant.* II.244), his gallantry (*Ant.* II.262) and his power to perform miracles (*Ant.* II.272ff.). The biblical narrative is in places amplified with legendary tales extolling his wisdom or courage or wondrous character. In this last connection the story is told how the Egyptian princess who adopted him brought the child to the Pharaoh and laid him in her father's arms, suggesting that he might be recognized as heir to the throne. As he hugged the child,

3

to please his daughter he placed his diadem on the boy's head, whereupon the young Moses tore it off and flung it to the ground where he trampled it underfoot (Two *midrashim* say he snatched the diadem from the king's head). 'This', says Josephus, 'was taken as an omen of evil import to the kingdom' (*Ant.* II.233ff.). In other places the biblical narrative is expurgated and Moses is exonerated for misdeeds assigned to him there. Thus, no mention is made of his having slain an Egyptian; the reason for his having to flee from Egypt is put down to the hatred of the Egyptian people and the envy of the king (*Ant.* II.254f.).

(c) In the rabbinic literature

Another valuable source of evidence is the rabbinic literature which, in its written form, post-dates the intertestamental period but reflects an oral stage of development which may be used to cast light on the Judaism of those years. Of special interest are the *haggadic midrashim* (an exegesis or development of the biblical stories containing ethical and religious teaching and well spiced with folklore and legendary material) and the *targumim* (translations or paraphrases of the Hebrew scriptures for use in the synagogue services). In these and in other related sources the same trends appear – the patriarchs become the subject of story and legend in which their virtues are extolled far beyond the record of scripture.

Thus, Abraham from Ur of the Chaldees is miraculously rescued from a fiery furnace into which the Chaldean king had thrown him (in Hebrew the word '*ur* means 'flame') and he is rewarded by God for not taking part in idolatry. As a child, says a later legend, this same Abraham, under threat of death, had been hidden in a cave and fed by the angel Gabriel. He was indeed a wonder-child, for at the age of twenty days it was found he could both walk and talk! Much is said about the merit that accrued to Abraham (even his faith in God is so regarded) which more than made up for any misdemeanours on his part. Abraham himself was all-too-aware of this, as a third century AD midrash makes clear: the patriarch has a vision of the messianic age in which he sees God seated on his throne, with the Messiah on his right and Abraham himself on his left. When Abraham expresses misgivings that the place of honour has been given to the Messiah, God reminds him that he himself is sitting at the patriarch's right hand!

Many references are made in Jewish lore to the chastity of Joseph and his strength in resisting temptation. One of these concerns the spelling of the name 'Joseph' in Psalm 81.6 which introduces an 'h' between the first two letters of the word. This, say the rabbis, is a letter from the sacred tetragrammaton YHIH (for 'Yahweh') and is inserted into Joseph's name as a mark of esteem. Another version says it was done because Joseph, in a single night, had been able to learn from Gabriel all the seventy languages of the earth!

As for Moses, through him the law had been made known, not just the written law but the oral law as well, for together they contained and conveyed the one revelation of true religion. But not only was Moses responsible for receiving the law and making it available to Israel, he was responsible too for making it known to the whole Gentile world for, according to one tradition at least, it was Moses himself who translated it into the languages of the seventy nations on earth. The story of his assumption into heaven, after the manner of Enoch and Elijah, appears in several guises. According to Samaritan tradition he is to be the model of the coming *Taheb* or Messiah in fulfilment of the prophecy in Deut. 18.15 which speaks of the coming of 'a prophet like Moses'. Like Elijah, it is said elsewhere, he will return 'at the end of the days' (Mal. 4.4f.) or else they will make their appearance side by side (cf. Deut. Rabbah III.17; Matt. 17.3; Mark 9.4; Luke 9.30). (For a number of these illustrations I am indebted to Louis Ginzberg, *The Legend of the Jews*, Philadelphia 1909 and Martin H. Scharlemann, *Stephen: a Singular Saint*, Pontifical Biblical Institute 1968. For the use of rabbinic sources in the study of early Judaism see Jacob Neusner, *Judaism: the Evidence of the Mishnah*, Chicago and London 1981, and *Early Rabbinic Judaism*, Leiden 1975.)

2. Voices from the past

In his hymn 'in praise of famous men', Ben Sira does not confine himself to the patriarchs of old. Alongside them, indeed embedded among them, are the ancient prophets whom he likewise extolls:

Then the prophet Elijah arose like a fire
and his word burned like a torch . . .
May the bones of the twelve prophets revive from where they lie,
For they comforted the people of Jacob and delivered them with
    confident hope (Ecclus. 48.1).

Like the patriarchs before them, the prophets were highly honoured, although the stories and legends told about them in the literature of the time were somewhat more restrained. Already their books had been placed alongside the Torah and recognized as sacred scripture. They were men of God who spoke and wrote by divine inspiration and with divine authority.

(a) The Dead Sea scrolls

But to the men of the Qumran community, for example, there was much more in the prophetic writings than met the eye. This is brought out in a series of commentaries written by the community's leader, the Teacher of Righteousness. Of particular interest and importance are the commentaries on a number of prophetic books such as Habakkuk 1–2, Hosea and Nahum. In the first of these, for example, it is made abundantly clear that the words written by the prophet are not what they appear to be or even what the prophet himself imagined them to be. In fact they contain and conceal a hidden message waiting to be made known. They relate not to the events of Habakkuk's day, but to the times in which the Qumran community itself is then living! They refer to the future which is now present or is about to be revealed and point unerringly to the fast-approaching end! The prophet's words were a mystery to himself and to his readers, awaiting their interpretation to be made known by the Teacher of Righteousness under the inspiration of the Spirit of God.

(b) The pseudepigrapha

During this same period other books were being written, in Palestine and in the Dispersion, whose authors shared a somewhat similar conviction concerning the word of prophecy and the nearness of the end. Indeed many fragments and portions of them have been found among the Qumran scrolls. But their method of presentation was different. They actually wrote in the name of ancient worthies – patriarchs and prophets alike – who had featured prominently in Israel's history. Such books are commonly called 'pseudepigrapha', books written under an assumed name, many of them being of an 'apocalyptic' kind, revealing the mysteries of the universe and of the unseen world. Through these 'inspired writings', for so they believed them to be, their authors spoke a word from God to their contemporary situation and declared the coming triumph of his kingdom.

Sometimes the book is written in a narrative idiom after the style of the *haggadic midrashim* to which reference has already been made.

Accounts are given or comments made on scripture in the form of stories which add, subtract or adapt so as to enhance the reputation of the ancient hero or else to make the story more applicable to the issues of the day. A case in point is the Book of Jubilees, dating from the second century BC which takes the form of a revelation given by God to Moses at Sinai and uncovers past and future history culminating in the coming of the messianic kingdom. This is done in the shape of a commentary on Genesis and part of Exodus in which the figures of Abraham, Jacob and Moses, for example, are dealt with in a free way to suit the purpose of the author. So too with the Genesis Apocryphon from Qumran which, in a colourful way, embellishes the story of Abraham as recorded in Genesis 12–15. The Lives of the Prophets, dating probably from the first century AD, is a straightforward account of 'the names of the prophets, and where they are from, and where they died and how, and where they lie', except that legendary material concerning prophecies and miracles are included which are not to be found in the biblical narratives. So too in the Martyrdom of Isaiah where the prophet's death at the hands of Manasseh is told in legendary form. From the same century comes Pseudo-Philo's Book of Biblical Antiquities (*Liber Antiquitatum Biblicarum*) which picks and chooses its biblical material to suit its own purpose and concentrates on the period of the Judges which forms a paradigm for the days in which the writer is now living. Other illustrations of this narrative-idiom in which history is re-told 'with a purpose' by patriarchs and prophets are the Life of Adam and Eve, Joseph and Aseneth, IV Baruch, Jannes and Jambres, Eldad and Modad and the Ladder of Jacob some of which are to be dated after the end of the first century AD.

At other times the book may be written in a testamentary idiom where the ancient worthy addresses his 'last will and testament' to his offspring. By this means the actual writer can teach religious and ethical truths that are particularly applicable to the age in which he is then writing. There are many 'Testaments' of this kind, ranging from the first century BC to the second or third century AD, associated with the names of Job, Abraham, Isaac, Jacob, Moses, Adam and Solomon. The best known and most comprehensive, however, is the Testaments of the XII Patriarchs which, though Christian in its present form, probably originated in the second century BC. Here the twelve sons of Jacob (after the style of Jacob's last words in Genesis 49) address their last words to their children. In each testament historical, hortatory and prophetic elements combine to convey teaching and revelation which are particularly apposite to 'the last days' in which the writer believes himself to be living.

At yet other times the books are written in an apocalyptic idiom which may make use of narrative or prayer or hymn or testament and, by means of dreams, visions or angelic intermediaries, seek to disclose the hidden mysteries of God in the heavenly places and to indicate how these things impinge on this earthly life. These exalted men, in whose names the books are written, can see, as others cannot see, the broad sweep of history and catch a glimpse of the end-time when the promises made to the fathers will find their realization in the messianic kingdom and in the age to come. In so doing they see beyond this world into that other world of spiritual reality and are able to recognize the traffic between them.

The most significant among these is the Ethiopic Book of Enoch (I Enoch) which in its present form is a composite work extending from the third or second century BC to the first century AD. The reference in Genesis 5.24 that 'Enoch walked with God, and he was not, for God took him' was the occasion for many legends in Jewish lore claiming that Enoch, having been taken away from the earth by God, was shown the secrets of the cosmos, the predetermined course of history and the future of the world and mankind. This Enoch-tradition found varied expression in at least two subsequent books know to us as the Slavonic Book of Enoch (II Enoch) and the Hebrew Book of Enoch (III Enoch). Other books of an apocalyptic kind are the Jewish Sibylline Oracles, the Treatise of Shem, the Apocryphon of Ezekiel, the Apocalypse of Zephaniah, the Apocalypse of Abraham, II Esdras (=IV Ezra), II Baruch and III Baruch ranging from the second century BC to the second century AD. Within this same milieu we may count a number of those books in the other two categories listed above which, although they may not in their entirety belong strictly to the apocalyptic genre, nevertheless contain elements which relate them closely to the more clearly identifiable apocalyptic writings.

3. What's in a name? The phenomenon of pseudonymity

Reference has been made to the fact that most of the pseudepigraphical books are of an apocalyptic kind. These form a recognizable literary genre, making use of narrative, testament, hymn and prayer to record what are claimed to be secret revelations concerning the cosmos and 'the unseen world' made known by the agency of angels or by means of visions and dreams. These revelations demonstrate God's triumph over evil in its cosmic as well as in its historical manifestations and declare the redemption and restoration of all creation.

An intriguing feature of this literature is that, almost without exception, it is written pseudonymously in the name of one or other of the great heroes of Israel's past, normally a patriarch or a prophet. It has been claimed, in explanation of this phenomenon, that the authors by so doing sought to deceive their readers by making use of inspired men of the past whose reputations stood high in the eyes of the Judaism of that time. But it is hard to credit these writers with such naïvety or their readers with such credulity. Quite apart from that, there are fairly clear indications in the books themselves that the writers genuinely believed they were disclosing ancient secrets which did not simply originate in their own fertile minds, and their readers apparently accepted them equally as genuine revelations from of old. How, then, are we to explain this usage? Was it a mere literary device or was it something more? In seeking an answer to such questions certain factors should be borne in mind:

(i) According to Jewish tradition, prophetic inspiration had ceased with the prophets Haggai, Zechariah and 'Malachi' in the fifth century and the hope was envisaged that God would yet raise up a prophet like Moses (cf. Deut. 18.15) or send his prophet Elijah (cf. Mal. 4.5) before the end would come. This is indicated, for example, in I Maccabees 4.46, 9.27 and 14.41 where it is stated that prophets had 'ceased to appear'. The writer of II Baruch points to the same conclusion: the prophets, he says, are asleep (85.3).

(ii) The apocalyptic visionaries believed that they themselves were recipients of divine revelations. It may be that the descriptions they give of visions and dreams by means of which such revelations are given are part of a literary convention which successive apocalyptic writers copied. Nevertheless, there are clear indications that, in the case of some of them at any rate, their descriptions reflect an actual experience in which they believed themselves to be inspired by the spirit of God and thereby to receive revelations concealed from the ordinary run of men (see further D. S. Russell, *From Early Judaism to Early Church*, 1986, pp. 103ff.). This is most vividly described in IV Ezra 14.38–42 where Ezra, having drunk the cup of inspiration, is able to dictate aloud not only the books of canonical scripture but also the secret books of apocalyptic vision (see pp. 108ff.).

(iii) The patriarchs of old who, in the traditions of Israel, had come to be honoured as men of knowledge, wisdom and renown, were recognized as repositories *par excellence* of all knowledge. They had walked closely with God on earth, and some of them like Enoch, Elijah and Moses had actually been taken up to share in the heavenly mysteries.

(iv) In his visions and dreams the apocalyptic visionary saw the ancient patriarch or prophet being introduced to these mysteries and in so doing he was introduced to them himself. What the ancient worthy saw he himself was now seeing. They were sharing a common knowledge; they were recipients of a common revelation.

(v) In a very real way the seer was able, as such a recipient, to identify himself with the patriarch or prophet by reason of their sharing together those secrets hidden from others. For this reason the seer would find it difficult to separate his own person from that of his renowned predecessor. A good example of this is to be found in I Enoch 1.2 which reads: '*Enoch* a righteous man, whose eyes were opened by God, saw the vision of the Holy One in the heavens, which the angels showed *me* and from them I heard everything.' A. R. C. Leaney comments: 'Third person becomes first without regard for formal clarity, thus partly concealing and partly revealing the need of the writer . . . to lose himself in the person whose special knowledge he claims to record . . . A member of a people distinguished by a strong sense of the mutual inherence of the one and the many could in such circumstances feel without insincerity an identity with a representative person of his nation's past' (*The Rule of Qumran and its Meaning*, 1966, pp. 67f.).

(vi) The apocalyptic writers give the distinct impression that they are inheritors rather than originators of the secret revelations they are now disclosing in their books. In other words, they belong to a tradition within which the hopes and expectations they now express had been preserved and developed. It is true that essentially Jewish apocalyptic is a literary phenomenon, but it can hardly be doubted that it had a long oral tradition which is reflected in the Old Testament itself in such passages as Ezekiel 38–39, Zechariah 1–8, 9–14, Joel 3 and Isaiah 24–27. This secret tradition was traced back to some ancient worthy who was regarded as the fountain-head, as it were, of secret knowledge imparted to him by God. According to the Book of Jubilees, for example, Enoch, who had an intimate relationship with God, passed on his revealed knowledge to Noah who recorded this in secret books which were passed on to Shem (10.4) and in due course to Abraham and to Levi. This same 'device' of secret books is used again in I Enoch where, it is said, they are passed on from generation to generation (104.11) until they come into the hands of those in the final generation for whom they have been preserved (104.12). The apocalyptic seer, as the final representative of this secret tradition, now discloses its secrets which he himself has now recorded in the name of that tradition's originator or 'patron saint'. This disclosure is in itself a sign that the end is at hand.

(vii) As the last, then, in a long line of succession, the seer is able to serve as spokesman for the progenitor, the patriarch or prophet of old. Conversely, the patriarch or prophet, as the fountain-head of revealed knowledge, was the source of all such revelations of divine truth. Just as Moses was deemed to be the revealer of Torah in all the generations after him, so the ancient worthy was recognized as the revealer of divine secrets far beyond his own day and right up to the time of the end. Just as the Rabbis could say, 'Thus has Moses spoken', so the apocalyptist could write, 'Thus have our fathers revealed'. Revelations concerning the seer's own day with its signs of the approaching end, are not the seer's only, but the ancient worthy's in whose name he writes.

(viii) This sense of 'identity' between the seer and the man of old would no doubt be strengthened by another factor – a conscious sense of affinity between the two. It was no mere accident that the authors of I Enoch and IV Ezra, for example, wrote in the names of these particular worthies of the past. The former showed a cosmopolitan outlook in keeping with Enoch who might be described as the greatest cosmopolitan of antiquity, whereas the latter in places revealed a narrow nationalism which accurately reflects the outlook of Ezra himself.

(ix) Within the developing apocalyptic tradition there were in all probability certain identifiable 'deposits' associated with particular figures of the past. One of these is the figure of Enoch. The books called after his name, as we shall see, are a very 'mixed bag'. I Enoch in particular is a composite work, indicating diverse and complex material gathering round his name, some of it having association with religious thought far beyond the bounds of Israel. Another is perhaps the figure of Moses (together with Ezra, 'the second Moses'). As revealer of the law he is also revealer of the divine mysteries which are now being disclosed in 'the last days'.

The apocalyptic seer stands as spokesman, then, not only of personal revelation made known to him by divine inspiration, but also and above all of that tradition of revealed truth at whose source stand patriarch and prophet as chosen visionaries of divine wisdom and secret knowledge. Seen in such a light as this, the adoption of pseudonyms is not a deception or even a device but a declaration that the truth revealed of old has now reached its consummation.

II

In the Beginning: Adam

1. The Genesis story

It is generally agreed that in the story of Adam and Eve contained in Genesis 1–5 two sources of material are to be detected. One of these is the so-called Priestly or P source found in 1.26–30 and 5.1–5 within which there is a fluctuation in the use of the Hebrew word *'adam*. The main emphasis is on the species 'man' ('male and female he created them', 1.27; 5.2) rather than on any particular man, though it is also used as a proper name to indicate one, Adam, who was made 'in the likeness of God' and lived for 930 years (5.1, 3). Thus, Adam is 'the first-created', but is at the same time the representative 'man'. Not only is he the first man, he is also the first patriarch whose lineage passes directly through his descendants to Abraham, the father of Israel (cf. 1 Chron. 1.1, 24). Having been made in God's image and likeness, Adam is given authority and rule over the animal creation (1.26) and, in partnership with his wife, is bidden to 'be fruitful and multiply, and fill the earth and subdue it' (1.28). In all this he is blessed by God and no mention is made of his disobedience and sin.

The other block of material, which is considerably earlier, is that of the so-called Yahwist or J source contained in 2.4b–4.1 and in which a rather different picture is presented of the creation of *'adam* and his helpmeet. Here 'man' is formed from the dust of the earth; God breathes into him the breath of life and he becomes 'a living being' (2.7). In the Garden of Eden every prospect pleases: only the fruit of the tree of the knowledge of good and evil he is forbidden to eat (2.9,17). Failing to find a helpmeet among the animals which he names (2.18–20), he is given the woman, formed from one of his own ribs (2.21ff.). Tempted by the serpent, she in turn tempts her husband to

13

eat the forbidden fruit. At once, aware of their nakedness, they hide from God's presence (3.8). As a result of their sin God punishes the woman with the pain of childbirth. By the same token the ground is cursed and men must toil to eat the fruit of it (3.16ff.). Finally they are driven from the Garden and cherubim are stationed 'with flaming sword' to 'guard the way to the tree of life' (3.24).

It has been argued that 'two different myths, one about creation and the other about paradise, form the bases for the Yahwist's final narrative' (Robin Scroggs, *The Last Adam*, 1966, p.1). The creation myth emphasizes 'the first man's exalted stature and positive relation to God'. The blessings of procreation and fertility are divinely ordered and indicate God's intention in creating man. He is a unique creation, having become a 'living being' by the breath of God, whose authority and rule over the animals is demonstrated in his naming both them and the woman given to him.

The Paradise myth has a quite different emphasis. Man is capable of a knowledge which would make him independent of God. God wills for him only what is good, but man rebels against him. His sin carries with it inevitable punishment – arduous toil, painful procreation and exclusion from Paradise. As in the creation myth, he remains mortal, though reference to 'the tree of life' (3.22) may suggest that immortality may at some point have been within his reach.

When these two myths are brought together in the Yahwist's account, the form and function of the first man are essentially those set forth in the Paradise myth. He remains unique in God's creation and is to be treated with dignity and respect; but the deeper impression is of one who, though acquiring knowledge forbidden him by God, brings suffering, death and sin which he bequeaths to the whole human race.

Such myths have a long history behind them and may well go back as far as the second millennium BC. Our purpose here is to look rather at their continuation and projection into the post-biblical period and to see the important mythical, legendary and theological developments that took place then.

2. Sources in the pseudepigrapha

It is quite clear that speculation concerning Adam was widespread in the post-biblical period as can be illustrated from many references in the apocryphal and pseudepigraphical writings, the Dead Sea scrolls, the works of Philo and the writings of Josephus. Here we are concerned with the evidence of the pseudepigrapha in such writings as 1 Enoch, the Book of Jubilees, the Testaments of the XII Patriarchs, the Life of Adam and Eve (with the Apocalypse of Moses), IV Ezra, II Baruch, the Apocalypse of Abraham, II Enoch, the Apocalypse of Adam, the Testament of Adam, the Apocalypse of Sedrach and the Greek Apocalypse of Ezra whose dates extend from the second century BC to the second century AD and beyond.

The Life of Adam and Eve is of particular significance, indicating speculations to be found among some at least of the Jews, probably in Palestine, towards the close of the first century AD. It has come down to us in Latin and Greek texts which no doubt represent a Hebrew original. The Latin text now appears with the title 'The Life of Adam and Eve', and the Greek text with the title 'The Apocalypse of Moses' (a misleading title based on a preface to the text which is in all probability a later editorial addition). The two texts are closely related to each other, but contain several major variations.

In brief, they relate certain incidents in the life of Adam and Eve after their expulsion from the Garden of Eden and record certain revelations, instructions and exhortations on the part of one or other of them, usually when they are on the point of death. The accounts given correspond in part at least to the biblical story, but the work as a whole is in the form of a *midrash* or 'commentary' which ranges freely and expresses thoughts and beliefs which reflect the theological speculation prevalent at the time of writing.

The Life begins with Adam and Eve, driven out of Paradise, living in a tent and beginning to feel the pangs of hunger but finding nothing to eat (1.1–4.2). They resolve to repent in the hope that God will have mercy on them and make provision for them. As a penance they decide to stand up to the neck in water, she for thirty-seven days in the river Tigris and he for forty days in the river Jordan where the fish and even the waters themselves join in his mourning (4.3–8.3). After eighteen days Satan, in the guise of a glorious angel, appears to Eve and offers her food. She leaves the water and her repentance and comes to Adam who chastises her for being seduced again by Satan (9.1–10.4; cf. Apoc. of Moses 17.1). Satan then reveals why he has acted in this way: it is because he had refused to worship Adam at Michael's bidding, as a result of which he had been cast out of heaven. Adam, on hearing this, persists in his repentance, and the devil disappears (11.1–17.3). Eve acknowledges her errors to Adam and they separate, Eve going towards the west where she finds she is pregnant. Adam joins her and she bears a son they call Cain. Michael then provides Adam with seed and instructs him how to till the ground to produce food by which they and future generations may live (18.1–22.2; cf. Apoc. of Moses 29.3–6). This section concludes with an account of the birth of Adam's other children and the murder of Abel by Cain (23.1–24.4; cf. Apoc. of Moses 1.1–5.1).

In chapters 25–29 of the Life Adam recounts to Seth a vision in which he ascends to the heavenly Paradise where he sees the figure of God whose appearance is 'unbearable flaming fire', surrounded by thousands of angels. He tells Adam that he will die because he has disregarded the divine command; Adam pleads for mercy and God relents – his descendants will survive. Michael then takes him out of Paradise, touching the waters that surround it with a rod so that they freeze, thus giving free passage across (25.1–29.3; cf. Apoc. of Moses 27.1–29.6).

Chapters 30.1–44.5 (paralleled in Apoc. of Moses 5.1b–14.3) tell of Adam's final illness and the events that surround it. At 930 years of age he gathers his sons around him, for he is 'sick with pains'. He sends Eve and Seth to Paradise to try and obtain oil from 'the tree of his mercy' (identified with 'the tree of life' in Apoc. of Moses 28.2ff.) with which to relieve his suffering (36.1f.). On the way there they are attacked by a beast. They remonstrate with it and it responds mockingly with a human voice, but in the end withdraws from Eve and her son who are 'the image of God'. Continuing on their way, they meet Michael who bids Seth return and tell his father Adam that 'the span of his life is completed', for in six days' time his soul will leave his body. And so they return home, taking with them aromatic herbs. They tell Adam their news and he blames Eve afresh for bringing upon them 'a great wound, transgression and sin in all our generations' (44.2).

At this point the Apocalypse of Moses introduces material (15–30) which does not appear in the Life. Adam bids Eve tell all their children the story of her transgression and 'fall' from Paradise (14.3; cf. Life 44.3 where she has to tell it *after* Adam's death) and this she proceeds to do. Adam and Eve were tending their separate portions of Paradise when the devil entered and enlisted the help of the serpent to cast out Adam through his wife. Then Satan came to Eve 'in the form of an angel and sang hymns to God as the angels' (17.1; cf. II Cor. 11.14), tempting her through the mouth of the serpent to eat the forbidden

16

fruit and to persuade her husband to do the same. She did so and the eyes of both were opened to see that they were naked (15.1–21.6). Michael now announces the entry of God to Paradise, and 'the throne of God was made ready where the tree of life is' (22.4). He calls for Adam and pronounces judgment against him: the ground he tills will be cursed and the animals will rise against him. And as for Eve, she will suffer 'birth pangs and unspeakable pains' (25.1–3). At the command of God they are driven out of Paradise; the tree of life they desire must await the time of resurrection (28.4). And so they depart from Paradise, taking with them aromatic herbs (29.6).

The account of the Apocalypse of Moses continues with the story of the death and burial of Adam and Eve (31.1–42.2; cf. Life 45–48). As Eve is confessing her sin she sees 'a chariot of light (drawn) by four radiant eagles' (33.2). As she and Seth watch, they see one of the six-winged cherubim carry off Adam's soul for cleansing to Lake Acheron and from there to Paradise in the third heaven (37.3–6). The angels then bring Adam's body into Paradise where God gives a pledge that his sorrow will be turned into joy, that the seducer will be cast down and that he (Adam) will 'sit above him . . . on the seducer's throne'. Adam's body and that of Abel, which had lain unattended from the day of his murder, are prepared with 'cloths and oil of fragrance' and buried in their place, with the solemn promise of resurrection (38.1–42.2). Eve had prayed that she might be buried beside her husband and within six days her wish was granted (42.3–43.4).

At this point in the narrative an episode is recorded in the Life (49.1–50.2) which has no parallel in the Apocalypse of Moses. It tells how, six days after Adam's death, Eve calls together her children and bids them record on tablets of stone and of clay the story of their two lives so that they will survive any future judgment by water or by fire. On her death Eve is buried: her family is bidden not to mourn beyond six days for 'the seventh day is a sign of the resurrection' (51.1–3; cf. Apoc. of Moses 43.1–4).

There is quite an extensive 'Adam literature' in addition to these writings, much of which goes well beyond the period with which we are dealing. The Apocalypse of Adam for example (to be dated some time between the first and the fourth centuries AD) is a gnostic document containing a revelation made known by Adam, just before his death, to his son Seth whose descendants represent the gnostic 'race'. The book makes little or no reference to the biblical text, but expounds the story of the Fall along its own peculiar gnostic lines: in particular, Adam and Eve had been created one androgynous being and were 'like the great eternal angels', but the creator (lesser) God had separated them so that their glory deserted them only to find its way into their 'seed' in the person of Seth and his descendants (1.7). Having narrated the story of the Fall, Adam is confronted in a vision by three 'glorious' men who reveal to him future events which he proceeds to describe to Seth. They concern a forecasting of the Flood followed by a re-allocation of the earth by Noah, and destruction by fire – vain attempts by the creator God to destroy the descendants of Seth. A deliverer now appears in the person of 'the Illuminator of knowledge' who is persecuted by 'the powers' of the world who are stirred up by 'the God of the powers' (6.1ff.). They are puzzled to know his origins as are 'thirteen kingdoms' each of which offers its own myth by way of explanation (7.1ff). But the race of Seth ('the race without a king') know and have been enlightened by him (7.49ff.). Their victory is assured and their standing is confirmed by a voice: they are 'those who know the eternal God (as distinct from the creator God) in wisdom of knowledge and teaching of eternal angels, for he knows all things' (8.1ff.). The book ends with a reference to 'holy baptism' which is here identified with 'secret knowledge' and may suggest that it was written in connection with a controversy over baptism between representatives of the Jewish community and the gnostic sect.

The Testament of Adam (second to fifth century AD) in its present form is a Christian redaction of a basic Jewish work or rather works. It consists of three parts: the Horarium, the Prophecy and the Hierarchy, the second of which shows the most distinctive Christian influence. In the Horarium Adam addresses Seth and tells him which parts of creation praise God each hour of the night (demons, doves, fish and fire, seraphim, upper waters, clouds, powers of the waters, grass, cherubim, human beings, the sun rising from Paradise and 'the waiting for incense', 1.1–12) and each hour of the day (the heavenly ones, angels, birds, beasts, heavens, cherubim, entry and exit from the presence of God, fire and waters, angels before the throne, the visitation of the spirit on the waters, the exultation and joy of the righteous, the entreaty of human beings to the gracious God, 2.1–12). Of particular interest is the reference to the praise of the seraphim in the fourth hour of the night: 'And so I used to hear, before I sinned, the sound of their wings in Paradise when the seraphim would beat them to the sound of their triple praise. But after I transgressed against the law, I no longer heard that sound' (1.4).

In the Prophecy, Adam again addresses Seth and tells him of his fall and the promise of his restoration and deification (3.2–4). He then forecasts the Flood brought about by the sins of the daughters of Cain. Six thousand years thereafter the end will come (3.5). Seth, having recorded his father's testament, tells of Adam's death and burial. The testament is sealed and placed in 'the cave of treasures' together with 'the offerings Adam had taken out of Paradise' (3.6).

The Hierarchy has no obvious relation to Adam. It enumerates nine different orders of heavenly powers together with their functions 'in the service and plan of this world'. These are (from the lowest to the highest): angels, archangels, archons, authorities, powers, dominions, thrones, seraphim and cherubim.

Different though they are in many respects, the three Adam books just noted (the Life of Adam and Eve together with the Apocalypse of Moses, the Apocalypse of Adam and the Testament of Adam) have a fair amount in common and illustrate both the continuity and the diversity of 'the Adam tradition'.

3. The first Adam

Between, say, the years 200 BC and AD 200 we find a considerable movement of thought on the part of the writers of the pseudepigrapha in their portrayal of the first man Adam and his wife Eve. The fact of their disobedience in eating the forbidden fruit in the Garden of Eden is taken seriously, not least in its effect on the whole human race through Adam, the representative man; but there also takes place a process of identification and glorification in which Adam, not least as representative and first patriarch of Israel, regains the glory he has lost and assumes the status of a heavenly being.

(a) As fallen man

The pseudepigraphical writers have some interesting, indeed penetrating, things to say about Adam as 'the representative man' through whom suffering and sin have become the lot of the human race.

On the day that Adam and Eve were expelled from the Garden of Eden it is said that the very birds and beasts who used to converse with one another in the Hebrew 'tongue of creation' (Jub. 12.26)

19

became silent (Jub. 3.28). The ground was cursed, toil became arduous and the animals rose up against them in disarray (Apoc. of Moses 24.1ff.). Untimely death came into being, affliction increased, illness was created, death was renewed, pride was stirred, passion was roused and goodness vanished (II Bar. 56.6). As for Adam, his body was submitted to 'seventy plagues': 'the pain of the first plague is affliction of the eyes; the pain of the second plague is of the hearing; and so one after the other all the plagues shall pursue you' (Apoc. of Moses 8.2). Only 'the oil of life' from the tree of life will be able to bring relief and prevent him from wasting away (Life 36.2).

And with suffering goes sin which is due to Adam's 'evil heart', the cause of so much misery to himself and his descendants. It is true that God gave Israel the gift of the Law, but 'he did not take away from them their evil heart . . . for the first Adam, burdened with an evil heart, transgressed and was overcome, as were also all who were descended from him. Thus the disease became permanent; the law was in the people's heart along with the evil root, but what was good departed, and the evil remained' (IV Ezra 3.19–22).

This 'evil heart', which is the fruit of the 'evil seed' (4.30) sown in Adam is to be identified with the *yeser ha-ra'* or 'evil inclination' which is spoken of in the rabbinic literature and in a number of the pseudepigrapha (cf. many references in the Tests. of the XII Patriarchs). Not only does it lead to alienation from God on the part of Adam; it affects likewise his descendants. 'O Adam, what have you done? For, though it was you who sinned, the fall was not yours alone, but ours also who are your descendants' (7.118). And so every nation, as a result of Adam's sin, walks after its own will and does ungodly things (3.7). Adam, then, is held responsible for the alienation of the whole human race, though nowhere is it clearly stated why there should be this connection between them.

Neither is it made clear in these writings how it is that, though Adam is held responsible by reason of the Fall (cf. Apoc. of Abr. 23), each man is nevertheless to be held responsible for his own sin (Apoc. of Abr. 26). The reason no doubt is that these were not regarded as contradictory at all, but rather complementary. Adam, by reason of the Fall, may be the primary source of darkness, but it is in the power of men to choose the light (II Bar. 18.1f.). Thus the freedom of men to choose their own destiny is set forth most cogently in II Baruch 54.15 and 19: 'For although Adam sinned first and had brought death upon all who were not in his own time, yet each of them who has been born from him has prepared for himself the coming torment. And further, each of them has chosen for himself the coming glory . . . Adam is, therefore, not the cause except only for himself, but each of us has become our own Adam.'

(b) As exalted man

But although the role of Adam as bearer of suffering, sin and death is fully recognized in these books, this is by no means the complete picture as presented by the writers of the pseudepigrapha.

Attempts are made, for example, to explain the origin of sin by some other means than by Adam's Fall and to excuse or even exonerate him for his act of disobedience. This is illustrated by the explanation sometimes given that sin and evil in the world are due to the evil designs of fallen angels called 'Watchers' who co-habited with 'the daughters of men' or to a rebellion in heaven itself on the part of Satan and his followers. But even where the 'Adam-theory' of the origin of sin prevails and Adam rather than the Watchers is held responsible, attempts are still made to pass the blame on and to lay it at the feet of either Satan or Eve or both together. This finds ample illustration in the Life of Adam and Eve (with the Apocalypse of Moses) where Satan, through the serpent, entices Eve who in turn tempts her husband to sin. Satan's motive in so doing is made clear: 'Adam, it is because of you I have been thrown out of (heaven). When you were created, I was cast out from the presence of God and was sent out from the fellowship of the angels' (Life 13.1f.). The reason for his bitterness is then made clearer still: Michael had commanded Satan to bow down and worship Adam who had been made in the image of God and set an example by doing so himself. Satan replies: 'I do not have to worship Adam . . . Why do you compel me? I will not worship one inferior and subsequent to me. I am prior to him in creation; before he was made, I was already made. He ought to worship me' (14.3; cf. Apoc. of Sedrach 5.2). And so now he plans to cast Adam out of Paradise just as he himself had been cast out of heaven and to do so through his wife (Apoc. of Moses 16.3).

But this does not exonerate Eve. She too is culpable and acknowledges her guilt, for she had willingly enticed her husband to eat the forbidden fruit (Apoc. of Moses 21.5). She readily confesses her sin and offers to take upon herself 'half the illness' which now afflicts him (Apoc. of Moses 9.2). It was she who had brought it upon him (Life 5.2) and fully deserved the chiding he gave: 'O evil woman! Why have

21

you wrought destruction among us? You have estranged me from the glory of God' (Apoc. of Moses 21.6). Any blessing she may receive is 'because of Adam' whose prayers for Eve were many (Life 21.2). Thus Satan and Eve take upon themselves much of the guilt of Adam whose reputation is salvaged from the ruins of the Fall.

A different picture of Adam is given by the writer of II Enoch for whom his creation is a perfect work of God: the seven components from which he is made and the seven senses by which he lives are the handiwork of the divine Wisdom itself (30.8f.). Even 'at his smallest he is great . . . like no other creature' (30.10). As Ben Sira had put it many years before, 'Adam (was honoured) above every living being in the creation' (Ecclus. 49.16). But, according to II Enoch, the honour went further still. God, says the writer, made Adam 'a second angel', set him up as a king (cf. also Jub. 2.14; IV Ezra 6.53f.; Apoc. of Moses 24.4) and conferred on him a glorious name: 'And on the earth I assigned him to be a second angel, honoured and great and glorious. And I assigned him to be a king to reign on earth and to have my wisdom. And there was nothing comparable to him on the earth among my creatures that exist. And I assigned to him a name from the four components: from East (A), from West (D), from North (A) and from South (M)' (30.11–13), each letter of his name being the first letter of the Greek words signifying the four main points of the compass. The 'four components' that constitute his name, like the 'seven components' that comprise his nature, demonstrate that he sums up in his own person the whole creation, a cosmos in miniature, a 'glorious man' indeed. But honour is conferred on Adam not only in the earthly but also in the heavenly Paradise. On arriving there, says II Enoch, 'the first sinner' is welcomed by 'the last righteous person', who makes up the roll of the elect, 'as a person invites his best friends to dinner with him and they arrive with joy' (42.5).

In the Testament of Abraham that joy is tempered with sorrow. In the realm of the departed this 'wondrous man . . . adorned in glory' is 'seated on a golden throne' and before him are two gates, one broad and one narrow. When he sees many souls passing through the broad gate, he cries and wails; and when he sees them passing through the narrow gate, he 'rejoices and exults' (11.1ff. Recension A; 8.1ff. Recension B). So too in the Life of Adam and Eve, Adam is carried off into 'the Paradise of righteousness' in the third heaven and into the presence of God himself (25.3). There the sun and moon pray for him (Apoc. of Moses 36.1) and he is assured that his sorrow will be turned into joy and he will take his place 'on the seducer's throne' (39.3). Eventually he will come forth from Paradise and be raised in resurrection: he will be given to eat of the tree of life and will be immortal forever (28.4). This last reference finds echo in the later document, the Testament of Adam, where the deification of Adam is clearly expressed. There the voice of God comes to him in the earthly Paradise: 'Adam, Adam, do not fear. You wanted to be a god; I will make you a god, not right now, but after a span of many years' (3.2; cf. John 10.33–36). In the earthly Paradise and in the heavenly he is recognized, then, as a man of great honour and renown.

It will have been observed that on a number of occasions the words 'wondrous' and 'glorious' are used to describe Adam. He is one who is at home in the company of 'the glorious angels' and shares in the glory of God himself. Indeed this is the destiny of all the righteous of whom Adam, 'the first created', is the forebear and prototype. Man is destined to be changed 'from beauty to loveliness, and from light to the splendour of glory' (II Bar. 51.10) and so become like the angels in heaven (I En. 69.11). 'Adam' is thus the image, not only of God in the first creation, but also of a new humanity in the new creation soon to be. This is well illustrated in the dream vision contained in I Enoch 85–90 where there is a direct continuity between the righteous Adam, under the figure of 'a white bull', and the future new community whose members are transformed into the same likeness at the coming of the Messiah and his kingdom (85.3ff.).

Thus, the end-time returns, as it were, to primordial time, to the generations of Adam before he sinned, and the primitive righteousness of Eden is at last restored. This correspondence between the Beginning and the End is a frequently recurring theme in these writings. Sometimes the Paradise-to-come is earthly (cf. Test. of Levi 18.10f.) and belongs to the original works of creation (cf. Jub. 2.7; II En. 30.1; IV Ezra 3.6, 6.2f.); at other times it is other-worldly, the dwelling-place of the righteous (cf. I En. 61.12; II En. 8.1ff.; II Bar. 4.3; IV Ezra 6.27 etc.) or else it may be a conflation of the two. Whatever its form may take, Adam 'the first-created' is seen as the prototype of that new creation brought about by God in which all the righteous at last will share.

III

Two Antediluvian Heroes: Enoch and Noah

1. Two men who 'walked with God'

Many antediluvian names are quoted among the early biblical heroes – Adam, Abel, Shem, Seth, Methuselah, Melchizedek – but none receives the honour given to Enoch who, together with Noah, is praised to the highest heavens as a man of righteousness and wisdom who found favour supremely in God's sight. The literature of early Judaism makes frequent reference to him as do later writings, Jewish and Christian alike. No doubt, the seed-bed, as it were, for much of this growth of interest is to be found in the intriguing passage in Genesis 5.21–24 which reads, 'When Enoch had lived sixty-five years, he became the father of Methuselah. Enoch walked with God after the birth of Methuselah three hundred years, and had other sons and daughters. Thus all the days of Enoch were three hundred and sixty-five years. Enoch walked with God; and he was not, for God took him.'

As we shall see, this miraculous entry of Enoch into heaven opened the way for all kinds of speculation concerning that spiritual world where God lives together with his hosts of angels. But there is good reason to believe that behind the biblical account itself, preserved by the Priestly writer of this part of Genesis, there lay earlier traditions still. Of particular interest is the early Babylonian tradition which tells how, in the time before the Flood, there were ten 'kings' who reigned for specified periods of time. These kings were semi-divine beings who had come down from heaven. The seventh in line was called Edoranchus who is no doubt to be identified with Enmeduranki, king of Sippar, which is known to us from other sources as the city of the sun-god Shamash. According to one authenticated source, this god

24

introduced Enmeduranki to the secrets of heaven and earth and taught him the art of divination. Having acquired this heavenly lore from the gods he became the founder of a guild of priestly diviners, passing on his secret knowledge to his descendants.

There can be little doubt about the connection between this Babylonian tradition and the Hebrew tradition concerning Enoch, the counterpart of Enmeduranki, as this is set out in the biblical account and in the post-biblical traditions of early Judaism. Thus, as Enmeduranki was the seventh in line from the first 'king' after creation, so Enoch was the seventh in line from Adam, the first man; the duration of Enoch's life is given as 365 years which is the same number as the days of the solar year and has a particular relevance to Enmeduranki who worshipped the sun-god; Enmeduranki's introduction to 'heavenly secrets' is reflected, as we shall see, in Enoch's heavenly journeys and his revelations of divine mysteries; the mythical, other-worldly, semi-divine character of the 'kings' may be reflected in the apotheosis of Enoch and his identification with a heavenly being (cf. I Enoch 71.14). At a more general level it may be noted that, in both Babylonian and Assyrian sources, the belief is expressed that the men who lived in antediluvian times were men of great knowledge and profound wisdom, a belief expressed also in the Jewish traditions concerning Enoch and others who, like him, lived before the Flood.

Among these 'others' is Enoch's great-grandson Noah who is described in scripture as 'a righteous man' and who, like Enoch, 'walked with God' (Gen. 6.9). His righteousness is again singled out for special mention in Ezekiel 14.14 and 20 where Noah is said to share this quality with two other ancient worthies, Daniel and Job, and also, as we shall see, in the post-biblical writings.

Here again, as in the case of Enoch, the influence of earlier Babylonian tradition may be detected. According to the Babylonian priest Berossus (third century BC), the tenth of the 'kings' who reigned before the Flood was one called Xisuthros in whose time the great Deluge took place. This name corresponds to the Babylonian form Atra-hasis (= Utnapishtim in another tradition) who was highly favoured by the god Enki (or Ea). Enki warned him to build an ark in view of the pending disaster that would come upon the earth. There can be little doubt that this Babylonian tradition lies behind the biblical account and that Noah, the tenth after Adam, is the counterpart of Atra-hasis, the tenth of the 'kings'. Like Atra-hasis he enjoys fellowship with his God, finds favour in his eyes and is given warning of the coming Flood.

The continuing and growing interest in these two antediluvian heroes is made perfectly plain in the voluminous Jewish literature of the post-biblical period, especially in those books commonly called 'pseudepigrapha'. Of particular importance in this regard are the first and second Books of Enoch, the Book of Jubilees and the Genesis Apocryphon from Qumran. These reveal a 'secret tradition' associated with the name of Enoch which is both composite and highly complex. Based on the simple assertion concerning Enoch in Genesis 5.21–24, it develops this in a highly speculative way in a tradition which was no doubt shaped and re-shaped orally for some time before finding written form in the Jewish literature of the second century BC onwards. Examination of the text of I Enoch indicates that at one time there may well have existed a separate 'Noah tradition' contained in an Apocalypse bearing his name and that elements of it have come to be incorporated in I Enoch itself.

In the following pages we shall try to assess developments within the Enoch tradition (and within that the Noah tradition) in the post-biblical Jewish literature. But first we must look at the contents of those books that bear Enoch's name and that provide us with our chief source of information.

2. The Enoch literature

This is contained in the First (Ethiopic) Book of Enoch (supplemented by the Book of Jubilees), the Second (Slavonic) Book of Enoch and the Third (Hebrew) Book of Enoch, the last of which lies well beyond our field of concern and may belong to the fifth or sixth century AD.

I Enoch is a composite work in five main parts ranging in date from the early second century BC to the first century AD. Most of the traditional material contained in these five sections or books was composed in Aramaic, a claim which has found substantiation in the Dead Sea scrolls from Qumran where Aramaic fragments or larger portions have come to light for every section apart from the so-called Parables of Enoch contained in chapters 37–71. Besides these, large Greek excerpts have been preserved in Syncellus and a number of Greek manuscripts have come to light over the past hundred years or so. The Greek translation of the original Aramaic was itself, in all probability, translated into Ge'ez, the language of ancient Ethiopia, in which several different manuscripts are available. The Book of Enoch is held in high regard by the Ethiopian church today where it is recognized as part of holy scripture.

It is clear that I Enoch, as it stands, represents the deposit of a long and complex tradition, part of which does not relate directly to Enoch himself, which has gathered round this ancient man of renown. R. H. Charles has argued that, in its present form, it incorporates (together with the Book of Jubilees) other material relating to Noah which may well at one time have had an independent existence as an Apocalypse of Noah (cf. I En. 6–11; 54.7–55.2; 60; 65.1–69.25; 106–107 and Jub. 7.20–39; 10.1–15). This finds some external support in the scrolls among which fragments of the 'Noah sections' have been found, written not in Aramaic, as are the other portions, but in Hebrew. Be that as it may, it is certain that Noah and Enoch belong closely together within this complex apocalyptic tradition.

The Book itself, in its final form, is artificially contrived to form five books, perhaps on the analogy of the Pentateuch or the Psalms. These are generally identified as the Book of Watchers (1–36), the Book of Parables or Similitudes (37–71), the Book of Heavenly Luminaries (72–82), the Book of Dream Visions (83–90) and the Book of Admonitions (91–105) followed by a conclusion in chapters 106–108.

(i) The Book of Watchers (1–36) is one of the earliest sections and is probably to be dated in the first quarter of the second century BC. In the first five chapters, which may have formed an introduction to the whole work, the author presents himself as God's spokesman and prophet by claiming a divine revelation through a vision in which he foresees the judgment of the wicked and the justification of the righteous. This indeed is to be a recurring theme throughout the entire work.

In the succeeding chapters (6–11) no reference is made to Enoch and the story is composite in character. It tells how two hundred angels or 'Watchers', under the leadership of Semyaza and Azazel 'lusted after the beautiful daughters of men' who bore children by them. These children grew up as giants who, together with their sires, corrupted the earth, teaching men to make instruments of war and all kinds of enchantments. Michael and his fellow-archangels intercede on behalf of mankind and in response to their plea God sends Sariel to warn Noah of the impending flood and bids Raphael to bind Azazel hand and foot. Gabriel and Michael are then bidden to bind and destroy the children of the Watchers whose doom is declared. Then shall the earth be cleansed and the messianic age begin (6–11).

Enoch now appears on the scene. He is bidden go and pronounce judgment on Azazel and the fallen angels. Hearing him in fear and trembling they beg him to intercede for them. In reply Enoch reminds the Watchers of the place they have left behind and warns them that they will have 'neither peace nor forgiveness of sin'. Their petition for mercy will not be granted. Then in a vision he is shown the glories of heaven and enters into the house of God and thereafter into a second house more glorious than the first in which is the throne of God. There he is bidden to return to the Watchers with further reproof, telling them that from the bodies of their giant offspring evil spirits will proceed which will 'work devastation on the earth' and they will have no peace until the day of final judgment (12–16).

In the remaining chapters Enoch is taken by angels in vision to the east, to the place of punishment for the fallen angels and finally to Sheol itself where the dead are separated into compartments corresponding to the degree of reward or punishment they will have to receive. The scene changes again and Enoch is taken to 'seven magnificent mountains' (24.2) where stands the throne of God (24.3; 25.3) and is shown a tree 'beautiful and fragrant' which is the tree of life. In the final chapters, in the east Enoch sees 'the garden of righteousness' (32.3). He is then taken to the north to 'the three gates of heaven' and to the west and south to the very ends of the earth. As he sees the wondrous works of God he blesses 'the Lord of Glory who has made great and glorious wonders' (17–36).

(ii) The Parables or Similitudes of Enoch are contained in chapters 37–71. Like some of the other books in I Enoch, the Parables were at one time an independent writing as the introduction in 37.1–2 suggests. Their date of origin is extremely difficult to determine, but the weight of scholarly opinion would seem to suggest some time in the first century AD.

Following an introductory chapter (37) the book relates three 'Parables' which in each case takes the form of a vision in which Enoch is transported from earth to heaven. These are contained in chapters 38–44, 45–57 and 58–69, with chapters 70 and 71 forming an epilogue (or epilogues) which may be additional to the rest of the book.

In the first Parable (38–44) Enoch sees in vision the coming judgment of the wicked. The righteous, who are God's 'chosen ones', appear and with them a supernatural being called 'the Righteous One' or 'the Chosen One' with whom they have an obvious affinity. As a prelude to a second vision a whirlwind carries Enoch off to heaven, to 'the dwelling of the righteous and the resting-place of the holy' (39.4) where the angels pray for the sons of men. Enoch rejoices and praises the name of the Lord (39.9ff.). At this point he sees thousands upon thousands of angels and four archangels whose names are revealed to him: Michael, Raphael, Gabriel and Phanuel (40.1ff.). He is shown 'all the secrets of heaven' (41.1) including the blessings of the righteous and the judgment of the wicked (41.1ff.), the secrets of the lightning and the thunder, the chambers of the sun and the moon, the division of the spirits of men (40; 41.3–9) and the identity of the stars and the angels (43–44). An interpolated poem on Wisdom tells how she was driven from earth and took her seat in heaven among the angels (42.2).

The second Parable (45–57) begins with a reference to the coming day of judgment when 'the Chosen One will sit on the throne of glory' as judge (45.3). The 'chosen ones' will dwell in a transformed earth 'in eternal blessing and light', but the sinners will be utterly destroyed (45.4–6). Four 'vignettes' of this 'Chosen One' are now presented:

In the first, following the scene depicted in Daniel 7, Enoch sees 'one who had a head of days' and another 'whose face had the appearance of a man . . . like one of the holy angels' (46.1). He is 'the one who has righteousness and with whom righteousness dwells', God's 'Chosen One' who is able to reveal 'all the treasures of what is secret' (46.3). 'This son of man', as he is called, will judge the kings and the mighty (46.4ff.), and the prayer of the righteous for vengeance will hasten their demise (47.1ff.).

In the second the scene changes at 48.2 and there takes place the naming of 'the son of man' who had been 'chosen and hidden' before the world was created. His qualities are described in terms reminiscent of God's Servant in Deutero-Isaiah – 'the light to the nations' who keeps safe the lot of the righteous (48.4,7). 'The kings of the earth' who have dealt cruelly will be given over into the hands of God's chosen ones (48.9) because they 'denied the Lord of Spirits and his Messiah' (48.10). Having extolled further the 'Chosen One' in whom dwells the spirit of wisdom (49.3), the seer describes the repentance of some on whom the Lord of Spirits shows mercy (50).

In the third the resurrection of the righteous at the end-time is foreseen when the Chosen One will be enthroned and the righteous will inherit the earth (51).

29

In the fourth, in pictures reminiscent of the Book of Watchers, Enoch in vision sets off on a journey to 'metal mountains' whose secrets 'serve the authority of (God's) Messiah' (52.4). Metals used in war will be done away when the Chosen One shall appear (52.8–9). 'Gifts and presents' are brought to him, but the wicked perish in 'deep valleys' at the hands of the 'angels of punishment' (53.1–54.6). Following an interpolation concerning judgment by the Flood (54.7–55.2), the theme of punishment continues, this time of Azazel and his hosts (55.3–56.4). And so the Parable ends with the return of God's people to Jerusalem 'from the east and from the west' (57).

The third Parable begins at chapter 58 and continues to chapter 69. There would appear to be some dislocation of the text, as elsewhere in I Enoch, and interpolations from a Noah tradition. It begins with a description of the blessedness of 'the righteous and chosen' (58.2) following the judgment, and a revelation of more celestial secrets (59.1ff.). In a Noachic interjection the Head of Days is seen seated on his throne and judgment is declared against two monsters, Leviathan and Behemoth which are cast, one into the sea and the other into the desert (60.7ff.), and further reference is made to the secrets of heaven (60.11ff.).

In 61.1–5 the angels make preparation for the glorification of the righteous and praise the Lord of Spirits who places the Chosen One 'on the throne of glory' where he will judge the angels (61.8) and thereafter the kings and the mighty who will see 'that son of a woman (or son of man) sitting on the throne of (God's) glory' (62.5). But the righteous will be saved and will eat with 'that son of man' (62.14) when they rise in resurrection (62.15f.); but the others will be driven from his presence (63.6).

In chapters 65–68, also from a Noachic source, Enoch tells Noah of the coming Flood, his own preservation and the work of the punishing angels. The rebellious angels are named (69.2ff.) and reference made to a mysterious oath which contains God's (?) 'secret name' (69.14f.). The Parable concludes with an exclamation of joy at the revelation of 'the name of that son of man' who sits on 'the throne of his glory'; all judgment is given to him, for 'evil will pass away' (69.26ff.).

In chapters 70 and 71 we come to the climax of the book, at least in its present form. In chapter 70 Enoch is 'lifted to the presence of that son of man' on 'chariots of the spirit' (70.1f). But in chapter 71 the writer goes further than this. Having ascended into heaven, where he is greeted by myriads of angels, Enoch's 'whole body melted' and his 'spirit was transformed' (71.11). Just then an angel steps forward and announces to Enoch: 'You are the son of man who was born to righteousness . . . and the righteousness of the Head of Days will not leave you' (71.14). For the righteous there will be 'length of days with that son of man' and they will have peace for evermore (71.17).

(iii) The Book of Heavenly Luminaries is contained in chapters 72–82 and may be one of the oldest sections of the Book of Enoch, dating from the early years of the second century BC or even earlier. Fragments found at Qumran confirm the view that what we now have is a shortened version of a longer text. It is an astronomical treatise dealing with the measurement of time based on the movement of the sun, the reliability of the solar year of 364 days and an account of cosmic upheavals marking the time of the end.

The form taken by these chapters is again that of a 'guided tour' through the heavens during which the archangel Uriel shows Enoch the 'gates' by which the sun, moon, stars and winds make their exits and their entrances and instructs him concerning the order and governance of their ways (72–79). This order and governance will be completely upset in the last days when there will be grave disorders on earth and among the heavenly bodies (80.2–8), and the heavenly tablets on which are written 'all the deeds of mankind' will be opened (81.1–2). Enoch is bidden to record these things and communicate them to his son Methuselah (81.5) so that he may deliver them to future generations (82.1). Blessings are recounted of those who know the right reckoning of the years to which reference is again made in terms of intercalary days and the movements of the stars (82.2ff.).

(iv) The Dream Visions, contained in chapters 83–90, are to be dated in the Maccabean period towards the end of the 160s BC. They consist of two visions granted to Enoch concerning the future of the world. The first is in chapters 83–84 and foretells the destruction of the earth by flood, caused by sin and traceable to the machinations of the fallen angels. The second (85–90) discloses the history of the world from the time of Adam right up to the time of the Maccabees and the coming of the messianic kingdom. It does this in the form of symbolic imagery in which the patriarchs are represented as oxen, the loyal Israelites as sheep and the heathen as wild beasts and birds of prey. The narrative of the 'sons of God' mating with the 'daughters of men', as outlined in Genesis 6.1–4, is now depicted in terms of 'fallen stars' symbolizing angels. These descend from heaven, become bulls, mate

31

with the heifers (women) and produce giants which are depicted as camels, elephants and asses (86.1–6).

Just then four men in white, representing four archangels, appear to Enoch and lift him up to 'a lofty place' high above the earth (87.1ff.) from where he is able to see the punishment of the fallen angels (88) together with the judgment of the Flood (89) and the subsequent period of Israel's history (89.10–90.12) which concludes with an attack by the Gentiles on the Jews (90.13–19).

God appoints seventy 'shepherds', guardian angels of Israel, to 'pasture the sheep' until the time of the end (89.59). He tells them how many sheep they may allow to be destroyed (89.60). But they exceed their authority and slay more than had been permitted (90.17) with the result that they receive punishment at the hands of God (90.25). At the same time judgment falls on the fallen angels and on the apostates (90.21–22). Then comes the new Jerusalem ('a new house', 90–29), the conversion of the remaining Gentiles ('all the wild animals and all the birds of heaven', 90.33), and finally the appearance of the Messiah himself ('a white bull was born and its horns were big', 90.37).

(v) The Book of Admonitions (91–105) may reflect the situation prevailing in the late Hasmonean period. It is addressed by Enoch to his children, and hence by the author to his contemporaries, admonishing them to follow righteousness and predicting their resurrection and the judgment of the wicked (92.1–5; 91.1–11, 18–19).

At this point there is introduced the so-called Apocalypse of Weeks (93.1–10; 91.12–17) received by revelation through the agency of an angel and confirmed in 'heavenly tablets' (93.1–2). History from Enoch's day to the coming of the end is divided into ten (seven plus three) unequal parts called 'weeks'. The first seven correspond to the periods of Enoch, Noah, Abraham, Moses, the Temple, Elijah and an 'apostate generation' (93.1–10); in the eighth week the righteous triumph over the wicked; in the ninth week righteous judgment is made known to the whole earth and evil vanishes from the world; and in the tenth week the climax comes with the judgment of the rebel angels and the creation of new heavens in an age that will have no end (91.12–17).

More admonitions are addressed to the righteous (94.1–5), followed by a series of 'woes' against the 'sinners' and a description of the judgment that will befall them. The sins attributed to them are partly of a religious kind – idolatry, blasphemy and perversion of the Law of God (99.7; 94.9; 99.2), and partly social, illustrating the pressures of the rich on the poor (94.6–7). The righteous are exhorted to fear God (101), having in mind the day of judgment (102.1–3). The wicked will suffer judgment (102.5), but the righteous will rejoice in resurrection (103.4). Divine retribution has already been recorded by the angels (104.1). The righteous must find assurance in this; in due course they will become 'associates of the host of heaven' (104.6).

The book ends with an assurance that the writings of Enoch will counteract evil teachings. They will be given to the righteous and the wise and be 'the source of joy and truth and much wisdom' (104.12) as well as a testimony to 'the sons of the earth' (105.1).

(vi) The conclusion (106–108) is an addition in two parts. Chapters 106 and 107 are from the Book of Noah and describe the birth of Noah as a wonder-child who is 'like the children of the angels of heaven, of a different type and not like us' (106.5). An appeal is made to Enoch 'whose dwelling is with the angels' (106.7) to explain this thing. In reply Enoch foretells the Flood and the evil that will precede it (106.14ff.); but Noah and his family will be saved (106.16). Chapter 108 forms a second addition which acclaims the punishment that will befall the wicked and the blessedness that will be the lot of the righteous.

The Second (Slavonic) Book of Enoch has survived in Slavonic in a longer and a shorter recension. Scholarly opinion is divided in respect of the relative value of these just as it is over the date and place of origin of the book. It may be tentatively suggested that it belongs to the intertestamental period and is of Jewish origin, emanating from some 'fringe' group. It has a two-fold theme: creation and eschatology. It covers the period from the time of Enoch to the time of the Flood but has no particular interest in history as such. In a number of respects its emphases are different from those in I Enoch, indicating that it did not belong to that particular line of tradition, although in terms of form and subject-matter there are distinct similarities.

The Book can be divided into three sections. After an introduction (1–2) in which Enoch narrates how he was taken up to heaven, there follows the description of a vision (3–37) in which he ascends through the seven heavens with their cosmological and eschatological mysteries (3–22) until at last he confronts the Lord seated on 'a supremely great throne' (22.2) where he becomes 'like one of the glorious angels' (22.10). He is bidden to write down what he has seen and heard, and this he does in 366 books (23.6). The Lord then recounts to him how, 'before anything existed at all', he constructed his creation (24–30). This sovereign Lord, for such he is, then discloses the coming of the Flood (34) because men reject his sole rule (34.1). Enoch is bidden to take back to earth the books he has written for the encouragement of the generation that will survive (35). He must expedite his commission, for in thirty days the Lord will take him back from earth to heaven (36–37).

In chapters 38–66 we have an account of Enoch's descent to earth and the instruction he has to give to his family which has a strong ethical ring about it. He claims divine authority for what is written (39) as he recounts the wonders of creation he has seen (39), together with the fate of the wicked in hell and the peace of the righteous in Paradise (42). The lessons of his vision are further spelt out (43–56): happy are those who bring help to the condemned and support to the needy, because on the day of judgment 'every weight and every scale will be exposed as in the market' (44.5). It is the Lord who repays (50.4). Blessings and curses will be meted out as they are deserved (52). Let them keep their hearts from every injustice (53.1).

Having addressed his children (38–56), he now addresses Methuselah and his brothers together with 'the elders of the people' (57–63), reminding them that they have responsibility to clothe the naked and give bread to the hungry (63.1). The scene changes and Enoch now addresses a crowd of two thousand men who had gathered to bid him farewell (64–66). He reminds them of this age and that which is to come, of the visible and the invisible creations and of the great judgment to follow. Let them guard their souls from every kind of evil and worship God alone (66.1–2). Having thus admonished them, Enoch is taken up by angels into heaven and the people glorify God (67).

The third section of the book is contained in chapters 68–73. Having offered sacrifices to God (68), the people express the hope that he will raise up a priest in succession to Enoch (69.2). In a dream Methuselah sees himself crowned for this office (69.5). The priestly line of succession from Methuselah to Melchizedek is then traced, and the narrative concludes with an account of Melchizedek's miraculous birth. This birth, it is said, took place without the agency of an earthly father, and the child was taken from the womb of his dead mother fully clothed and able to speak! Noah and his brother Nir who were in attendance dressed him in priestly garments and gave him the holy bread (71.21). Concerned about his destiny in an evil generation, they were assured that God would soon send Gabriel to remove him to the Paradise of Eden (71.28); Melchizedek would become 'the head of priests reigning over a royal people' (71.34). The book ends with the departure of Melchizedek to Paradise carried on Gabriel's wings (72.9).

3. The Enoch tradition (with Noah)

It is quite clear, from a reading of the Enoch literature, that there had grown up during the intertestamental period a considerable Enoch tradition which was far from homogeneous but which found its focus in the person of Enoch himself. Or, perhaps more accurately, there had grown up varied traditions loosely associated either with the name of Enoch or with speculations that had already attached themselves to him. These are well illustrated, as we have seen, in the books that bear his name, enhanced by traditions concerning Noah and supplemented in particular by material from the Book of Jubilees (cf. 4.17–25; 10.17; 19.24–27; 21.10). The picture of Enoch (and Noah) there presented may be summed up under several headings:

(a) A righteous man

Both men were highly honoured in the literature of the intertestamental period for many reasons, not least because of their righteousness in God's sight.

Ben Sira (c. 180 BC), for example, refers to Enoch as 'an example of repentance' (44.16), and the writer of the Book of Jubilees comments that he excelled all others 'because of the righteousness wherein he was perfect' (10.17). This is confirmed by the several books that make up I Enoch. There he is described as a 'scribe of righteousness' (12.4) who condemns evil and has the responsibility of recording God's judgment against the angel-Watchers who 'defiled themselves with women'.

Not only so, he is himself a teacher of righteousness. Thus, he urges his own children to 'love righteousness and walk in it; for the paths of righteousness are worthy of acceptance, but the people of iniquity will quickly be destroyed and vanish' (94.1; cf. 91.19). And to the righteous he says, 'Do not walk in the wicked path, nor in wrongdoing, nor in the paths of death . . . but seek and choose for yourselves righteousness and a life that is pleasing' (94.3f.); he exhorts them to fear God (101.1ff.), assuring them of the joy of resurrection (103.4) and of union with 'the host of heaven' (104.6). This same emphasis is made in the high ethical teaching Enoch gives to his family in II Enoch where, interestingly enough, several variant titles to the Book describe him as 'righteous Enoch'. He admonishes his family to guard themselves against evil and to accept responsibility not only towards the poor and hungry but even towards the animal creation (58–60). Elsewhere (in the Parables) Enoch has a particular affinity with 'the Righteous One', 'the Chosen One', in whom righteousness dwells (44.3) and indeed with all the righteous who will rise in resurrection (94.1–5, etc.).

In the Apocalypse of Weeks the righteousness of Enoch finds expression in his description of the coming kingdom: the eighth week is 'a week of righteousness' in which righteous judgment will be executed against those who do wrong; the ninth week will see the reward of righteousness over all the earth (91.12ff.); and the tenth week will witness the continuation of 'goodness and righteousness' for ever and ever (91.17). Elsewhere this idyllic future is depicted in terms of 'a garden' (77.4) or 'a spring' (48.1) of righteousness where 'the prayers of the righteous' ascend to the Lord of Spirits (47.1).

Alongside Enoch, Ben Sira follows up the biblical tradition (cf. Gen. 6.9; Ezek. 14.14,20) by singling out Noah as a righteous man who pleased God:

> Noah was found perfect and righteous;
> in the time of wrath he was taken in exchange;
> therefore a remnant was left to the earth
> when the flood came (44.17).

This is taken up and developed in other post-biblical writings, most fully in I Enoch, Jubilees and the Genesis Apocryphon from Qumran (see also II En. 35.1; IV Ezra 3.11). Thus he is declared to be 'pure and innocent' because, unlike the others who will be destroyed in the Flood, he has eschewed evil – 'all the secrets of the angels, and all the wrongdoing of the satans and all their secret power and all the power of those who practise magic arts and the power of enchantments and the power of those who cast molten images for all the earth' (I En. 65.6ff.).

He is one who speaks the truth (Gen. Apocr. VI.2) and in no way departs from what God has ordained for him (Jub. 5.19). Even at the time of his birth, it is said, 'he opened his mouth and spoke to the Lord of Righteousness' or, according to another reading, 'spoke to the Lord with righteousness' (I En. 106.3). His righteousness is revealed, moreover, in deed as well as in word, for he took to wife one of his own kinsfolk (Jub. 4.33) and so set an example to his descendants (Tob. 4.12).

But not only was he a righteous man in himself; he became a preacher of righteousness to others. The human race had become corrupt through the fallen angels and their evil progeny and so Noah, 'indignant at their conduct and viewing their counsels with displeasure, urged them to come to a better frame of mind and amend their ways' (Ant. I.74). Thus it was that he became the progenitor of all the righteous who survived the Flood (IV Ezra 3.11).

(b) A visionary

It is a common feature of the apocalyptic literature of the intertestamental period that the ancient worthy in whose name the particular book is written should claim to have received divine revelations in the form of a vision or a dream in which he is shown mysteries beyond human knowledge. Sometimes the vision takes the form of a heavenly journey into the immediate presence of God, or to the realms of the departed or to 'the ends of the earth'. More often than not the seer is accompanied by an angelic-guide who 'shows him round' and explains to him the strange and marvellous things he is privileged to behold. Ample use is made of symbolism and mythology, some of which is familiar to us from the Old Testament and some is culled from the syncretistic religious world in which the book was written.

The traditions associated with the name of Enoch admirably illustrate this pattern. He is presented as a visionary who is privileged to see what God has chosen to reveal to few among men. Nor is it surprising that one who 'walked with God, and he was not, for God took him', should lend himself to the idea of journeys, heavenly and otherwise, during which he receives divine revelations made known to him by angels and archangels. In I Enoch 6–36, for example, he is taken in vision to the heavens (in II Enoch they are seven in number), to the throne of God, and from there to Sheol where the souls of the dead await the final judgment, and then away to the ends of the earth.

These journeys of Enoch recall the journeys of the Babylonian hero Gilgamesh who visits Utnapishtim in the underworld and of Homer's Odesseus who travels to meet the shades of the departed in Hades. Much legendary material was ready to hand and is amply used by the writers of I Enoch. References, for example, to the 'seven magnificent mountains' in 24.2 and to the 'metal mountains' in 52.2, from which are made weapons of war, find echoes in popular mythology and seem to have association with astrological lore, whilst the mythical monsters Leviathan and Behemoth in 60.7ff. are familiar to us from the Old Testament (cf. Job 40.15–24; Pss. 74.14; 104.26; Isa. 27.1, etc.) and elsewhere in the post-biblical literature (e.g. IV Ezra 6.49f.). Such allusions are a reminder of the cross-cultural influences shaping the presentation of the figure of Enoch in the intertestamental years.

By such means as these, then, speculation upon speculation is added to the biblical story of Enoch, building up a picture of one who, by means of visions and the help of angels, is the recipient of revelations which few mortal men have ever seen.

(c) A revealer of divine secrets

But what are these revelations? They are divine secrets in the keeping of angels and archangels and may be revealed only to certain highly privileged people like the patriarchs of old whose lives have pleased God. Among the secrets revealed to Noah, we are told, is that of the art of healing because of his resistance to the demons who cause all kinds of ailments and diseases: 'And the healing of all their illnesses together with their seductions we told Noah so that he might heal by means of herbs of the earth. And Noah wrote everything in a book just as we taught him according to every kind of healing' (Jub. 10.12f.). This is in keeping with a belief expressed among the Essenes from whose secret books they learned the medicinal power of roots and the quality of stones. Another 'secret' made known to Enoch concerns the art of making instruments of war like swords, daggers, shields and breastplates and the dangers of allurements like bracelets, ornaments, costly stones and colouring tinctures (I En. 8.1).

Apart from these practical and 'down to earth' revelations, the secrets made known by the angels can be said to fall into three categories: the cosmological (or astrological), the theosophical and the eschatological. In particular they relate to the order of the universe, the mystical experience of God and the nature of 'the last things'.

The first of these is described in I Enoch, and again in II Enoch, and a careful account given of the natural elements and the movements of the heavenly bodies – not so much their beauty or even their wonder, but rather their order and their governance within the cosmos. Thus, the Book of Heavenly Luminaries (I En. 72–82) describes the movement of the sun through its twelve 'portals', the various phases of the moon and the paths taken by the stars, demonstrating that there is no deviation in the laws of the heavenly bodies. Only with the coming of the day of judgment will the order of the cosmos be upset, for then the moon will alter its course and the stars will fail to appear at their proper seasons (80.1ff.). A similar allusion is made in Jubilees 4.17, already quoted, where Enoch, it is said, records 'the signs of the heaven according to the order of their months', the reference being to the twelve months of the solar calendar corresponding to the twelve signs of the Zodiac whose meticulous observation and observance were crucial for the fixing of the religious festivals. We observe that the writers of these books were at one with the Qumran covenanters in advocating a solar calendar over aginst the lunar calendar of 'official' Judaism. This became an occasion of great conflict between the men of Qumran and the Jerusalem hierarchy, and no doubt Jubilees and I Enoch 72–82 reflect earlier stages in such a bitter quarrel.

Elsewhere, in the writings of Pseudo-Eupolemus for example (before the first century BC), it is stated that Enoch was the first to discover astrology. The writer recognizes that the Greeks bestowed this honour on Atlas; but that difficulty is easily resolved, for 'Atlas is the same as Enoch' (*Praeparatic Evangelica* 9.17.8f.)! In the following line such knowledge is said to come 'through the angels'. This agrees with such a passage as Jubilees 4.21 where it is said of Methuselah, Enoch's son, 'And he was with the angels of God six jubilees of years. And they showed him everything which is on earth and in the heavens . . . and he wrote everything down' (cf. I En. 106.13). Other legends associate Noah with Nimrod, the planner of the Tower of Babel, and with Bel and Kronos of Babylonian mythology, indicating that 'these (Enoch) legends had close affinities with mythological material of a Babylonian origin and that they were passed on as part of a living tradition' into Jewish thought and Jewish literature (See my *The Method and Message of Jewish Apocalyptic*, 1964, pp. 112f.). In this connection Martin Hengel comments: 'The essential feature in all these mythological speculations is that despite their gigantic nature, the ancestral deities of Babylon and Greece, Bel and Kronos, are mortal men. Their descendants are punished by God for their sins and scattered over the earth' (*Judaism and Hellenism*, vol. 1, 1974, p. 89). In such a way the pagan sagas are 'demythologized', their polytheism is debased and the biblical revelation confirmed.

Alongside this interest in cosmology, astrology and creation went an interest in theosophy and in particular revelations of secrets concerning 'the throne of God'. This concept no doubt finds its biblical origin in the heavenly Council described there (cf. Isa. 6) and more especially in the symbolism of Ezekiel 1 which describes the *merkabah* or chariot-throne of God, accompanied by 'living creatures darting to and fro, like a flash of lightning' (1.14ff.). Enoch's description is more elaborate still: 'And I observed and saw a lofty throne – its appearance was like crystal and its wheels like the shining sun; and (I heard) the voice of the cherubim, and from beneath the throne were issuing streams of flaming fire. It was difficult to look at it. And the Great Glory was sitting upon it . . . None of the angels was able to come in and see the face of the Excellent and the Glorious One' (I En. 14.18ff.). Here we see speculation building on the biblical material, speculation which is developed even further in 71.7 where Ezekiel's 'living creatures' are identified as seraphim, cherubim and ophanim 'who do not sleep, but keep watch over the throne of his glory' (cf. also 61.10). This contemplation on the *merkabah*, with God seated in glory, continues in the Hymns and Angelic Liturgy from Qumran and in the New Testament Apocalypse (4.3). Indeed, the search for mystical knowledge continued for centuries to come and is a prominent feature of mediaeval Jewish Kabbalist worship.

But perhaps the greatest secrets of all are those that relate to eschatology and predict the end-time. As the writer of Jubilees puts it, the divine secrets have to do with 'what was and what will be . . . as it will happen among the children of men in their generations until the day of judgment' (4.19). Enoch's journeys into the heavenly places show him the joys of the righteous and the plight of the wicked which are indications of the joys and sorrows yet to be revealed at the close of the age. The theme of the coming judgment is a constantly recurring one and is revealed to Noah, for example, in terms of the coming Flood (10.12) which is a paradigm of that final cataclysm when all evil will be destroyed and righteousness will be established in a new age that will last for ever (I En. 91.12–17).

Closely connected with these 'signs of the end' is the figure of Antichrist who is sometimes represented as a human being and at other times as Beliar the prince of demons. In three later writings (the Apocalypses of Daniel, Elijah and Zephaniah) it is interesting to note that Enoch appears with Elijah as God's champion and as a leading opponent of Antichrist at the end of the days.

Having received all these secrets, then, as divine revelations, Enoch is told to record them in a book and pass them on in the form of a secret tradition, first to Noah and then through him to succeeding generations: 'Thus, Enoch, the father of your father, commanded Methuselah, his son, and Methuselah (commanded) Lamech his son. And Lamech commanded me (Noah) everything which his fathers commanded him. And I am commanding you, my sons, just as Enoch commanded his son in the first jubilee' (Jub. 7.38f.). And so Noah wrote everything in a book which he gave to his son Shem (10.14) who passed the secrets on to Abraham who, according to tradition, studied in the school of Shem (cf. Pirke de R. Eleazer 8). Through Isaac and Jacob they came into the hands of Levi (45.16) with whose descendants they remain 'unto this day' (indicating no doubt that the author of Jubilees was himself a priest and a descendant of Levi, inheritor of 'the secrets of the Most High'). The same tradition is found in I Enoch (82.1) and again in II Enoch where, it is said, the secrets were reported in no fewer than 366 books (23.6).

Thus Enoch, the 'scribe of righteousness', is presented as Enoch the 'scribe of the secrets of God' who holds the key to the ordering of the universe, who has beheld the majesty of God seated on his glorious throne and who has caught a glimpse beforehand of the after-life and of the judgment and triumph of the age to come.

(d) A companion of angels

The 'righteous ones', of whom Enoch and Noah are outstanding examples, are to share in the glories of the after-life in which they will become 'associates of the (angelic) host of heaven' (I En. 104.6). More than that, they will actually 'become angels in heaven' (51.4) and have 'their dwelling with the angels and their meeting-places with the holy ones . . . petitioning and supplicating and praying on behalf of the sons of men' (39.5). Like the angels themselves, the righteous are God's 'holy ones', God's 'chosen ones', who can look forward to the time when 'the chosen' (on earth) will begin to dwell with 'the chosen' (in heaven) (61.4).

And if this is true of 'the righteous' as such, how much more obviously true is it of men like Enoch and Noah, so renowned for their righteousness. Enoch's dwelling-place is indeed 'with the angels' (12.2; 106.7) who reveal to him the secrets of God (40.2; 41.1), who rely on his intercessory prayers (13.6ff.) and who, in their fallen state, receive judgment from his mouth (13.8). And of Noah it can be said, 'He is not like a man, but is like the children of the angels of heaven, of a different kind, and not like us. His eyes (are) like the rays of the

41

sun, and his face glorious' (106.5). His birth, like that of Melchizedek (II En. 71.1ff.), was miraculous (I En. 106–107), and, like him also (II En. 72.9), he was permitted to enter into Paradise (I En. 4.23). Both men, by reason of their righteousness, belong to the company of God's holy and chosen ones on earth and in the angelic world beyond.

Of special interest in this connection are the references in the Parables of Enoch to a figure who stands before 'the Head of Days' (46.1) or is seated on the 'throne of glory' (45.3, etc.), reminiscent of the investiture scene in Daniel 7. He is called 'the Righteous One' (38.2; 53.6) or 'the Chosen One' (53.6, etc.) and is identified as 'the son of man who has righteousness, and with whom righteousness dwells' (46.3). Much has been written on the nature and identity of this 'son of man' and many problems remain. But a number of assertions, however tentative, can be made.

One is that the expression 'son of man' is not here a title alongside 'the Righteous One' and 'the Chosen One', but rather a simple designation meaning 'man', standing symbolically (as is common in this style of literature) for an angelic being 'whose face had the appearance of a man . . . full of grace, like one of the holy angels' (46.1) and referring back to 'the Righteous, Chosen One'.

Another is that this angelic being who is called 'Righteous' and 'Chosen' is the heavenly counterpart of 'the righteous' and 'the chosen' here on earth just as in the Book of Daniel the angels of Persia and Greece are counterparts of the earthly rulers of these respective worldly powers. Here in the Parables the 'son of man' figure represents not a nation or a people as such, but 'the righteous' to whom will be given the joys of the coming kingdom.

A third is that, in at least one reference, this angelic 'son of man' is actually identified with Enoch himself. This is in 71.14 which reads: 'You are the son of man who was born to righteousness' (R. H. Charles, in his translation, reads quite arbitrarily, 'This is the son of man,' etc.). There is, in addition, a disputed reading at 70.1 which says, with reference to Enoch, 'the name of that son of man was raised aloft . . . to the Lord of Spirits' which would tend to support the same idea. The reading given by Charles and Knibb, however, is to be preferred which does not make any such claim: Enoch's name is lifted up 'to the presence of that son of man *and* to the presence of the Lord of Spirits'. We are left, however, with the indisputable evidence of 71.14 and its identification of Enoch with the angelic 'son of man'. If this is so and if the identification of the 'son of man' with an angel is correct, we have here the belief expressed not only in his exaltation but also in his transformation (with this we may compare the appearance of Melchizedek in the Dead Sea scrolls as captain of the host of heaven, suggesting that he is to be numbered among the archangels, cf. 11Q Melch.)

Such an identification may not be as far-fetched as it might at first glance appear to be, having in mind the intimate relationship outlined above between 'the righteous Enoch' and 'the righteous ones' on earth, between 'the holy ones' on earth and 'the holy ones' in heaven, and between 'the Righteous, Chosen One' as 'son of man' and all the righteous on earth and in heaven. Just as the Righteous One as 'son of man' is counterpart of 'the righteous ones' on earth, so he may be regarded as the counterpart of their supreme representative, 'the righteous Enoch'. There are thus indications in the Parables themselves of the identification of Enoch with this 'son of man', but only in 71.14 is the claim categorically made. If, as may well be the case, this chapter comes from a secondary source and is an addition to the original text, it is nevertheless true to the spirit of the Parables as a whole. Enoch the righteous, through his visionary experience, has already entered into the secret presence of God where all the righteous are destined to be (62.14).

The exaltation of Enoch to the rank of archangel finds corroboration in the two later books that bear his name, II and III Enoch. In the first of these we read: 'And Michael extracted me from my clothes. He anointed me with the delightful oil . . . I had become like one of the glorious ones, and there was no observable difference' (22.9f.). Enoch, to all appearances, has become like Michael the archangel himself and will stand before God for ever (22.7). He subsequently returns to earth for the space of thirty days (36.1) and finally ascends to heaven to resume there his angelic role (36.1; 67.2). In III Enoch, which is to be dated well beyond the period of our present concern (fifth century AD?), we find a further development still. There Enoch is introduced with the name 'Metatron' – an archangel, no less, who is designated 'the lesser Yahweh' (12.5) to whom God reveals all the secrets of the cosmos (11.1).

But even within the intertestamental period itself, the figure of Enoch has come a long way from the simple, if mysterious, figure of Genesis 6.9 who 'walked with God . . . and was not'. His idealization and exaltation are complete.

IV

Daniel, the Wise Man

1. The name and its origin

It is generally agreed that the Book of Daniel, in the form in which it now appears, was written in the time of the Syrian tyrant, Antiochus Epiphanes, around the year 164 BC. The hero of the book is one, Daniel, a Jewish exile living in Babylon during the sixth century BC. The name is a fairly familiar one in the Old Testament. In I Chronicles 3.1, for example, it is given as the name of one of David's sons, and in Ezra 8.2 and Nehemiah 10.7 it is the name of a priest who returned to Jerusalem in the second half of the fifth century BC. Neither of these men corresponds to the hero of our book, nor does there seem to be any reason why their name should be adopted for the purpose of the stories told in it.

The fact is that, outside the Book of Daniel itself, we have no information about such an exile living at such a time. There is, however, one reference (to which allusion has already been made) which may provide a useful clue: Ezekiel 14.14 and 20 together with 28.3. In the first two of these verses Daniel is associated with Noah and Job, implying no doubt that, like them, he is an antediluvian hero; together they are praised for their righteousness and their powers of intercession. In the third of the verses the prince of Tyre is roundly condemned because, in his arrogance, he believed himself to be 'wiser than Daniel', suggesting that in this antediluvian Daniel we have the figure of a proverbially wise man. It is true that in Ezekiel the name is spelt 'Dan'el', without the 'i'; but there can be little doubt that this is a different form of the same name and is to be pronounced as 'Daniel'. These three men – Noah, Daniel and Job – renowned for their righteousness and outstanding wisdom, were not Israelite

44

patriarchs, but rather holy men belonging to other nations, and the impression given is that they are here figures in a tradition or traditions wider than those of Israel itself.

This impression is strengthened by the occurrence of the name 'Dnil' (which may be vocalized as'Dan'el' or 'Daniel'), borne by a king, in the Ugaritic 'Tale of Aqhat' discovered at Ras Shamra in northern Syria and dating from the fourteenth century BC. There it is said of him:

He judges the cause of the widow,
He tries the case of the orphan.

That is, he is a wise ruler, renowned for his righteous acts. Taken in conjunction with the Ezekiel references this would indicate that, from very early times, there was a Phoenician-Canaanite legend concerning an ancient hero whose reputation for righteousness and wisdom was such that he was designated a man of renown.

There are indications, moreover, which suggest that this old legend may well have survived in different forms in Jewish lore. For example, one development of it may conceivably be reflected in I Enoch 6.7 and 69.2 where 'Dan'el' or 'Daniel' is the name given to one of the fallen angels, the 'wisdom figure' of old having assumed angelic status and then subsequently 'falling from grace'. Another development may have gone in quite another direction, finding its locus in Babylon with its world-renowned reputation for wisdom and finding expression in a collection of stories concerning one whose wisdom confounded that of 'the wise'.

But is there any *proof* that the hero of the Book of Daniel may have been associated with the ancient Daniel and that the Ezekiel references in particular may have been used in this way? It has to be said that the evidence for such an identification falls short of actual proof; nevertheless, there are certain pointers in this direction which make such an assumption not just plausible but even probable. It can be clearly shown, for example, that the writer of the Book of Daniel was familiar with the writings of Ezekiel; in particular the vision recorded in Daniel 4.10–12 and 20, with its description of the tree, under whose branches the beasts and the birds find lodging, is dependent on the oracle contained in Ezekiel 31 which in turn is closely related to Ezekiel 28 where, at verse 3, Daniel is presented as 'a wise man'.

It has been suggested, moreover, that the absence of any genealogy associated with the name of Daniel in the book of that name may be of significance in this same connection. In Jewish tradition and Jewish writings, the recording of such genealogies is customary; its absence in the case of the Book of Daniel may suggest that we may be dealing here, not with a specifically Hebrew tradition concerning the man Daniel, but with a borrowed legendary figure.

Besides these 'pointers', there are at least another two indications in the literature of the intertestamental period which suggest a connection with the ancient legend of Daniel. One is the reference in Jubilees 4.20 which indicates that Enoch married Edni 'the daughter of Dan'el, his father's brother', i.e. Dan'el is the uncle and father-in-law of Enoch and the great-great-grandfather of Noah. The other is in Ben Sira 49.8f. (in the Hebrew text) where it is said that 'Ezekiel saw a vision . . . He also made mention of Job (among the prophets) who maintained all the ways of righteousness'. E. W. Heaton comments that it is significant that 'in his brief account of Ezekiel just those verses which refer to the three righteous men of old times' should be singled out (*The Book of Daniel*, Torch Bible Commentaries, 1956, pp. 25f.).

The cumulative evidence would indicate that during the intertestamental period, then, the story of an ancient hero, Daniel, renowned for his wisdom, was known in Jewish circles. Such knowledge was not confined, however, to the writings just mentioned. Indeed, there would appear to have been at this time a cycle of tradition concerning the man Daniel which found expression not only in the biblical narratives but also in the 'additions' to Daniel and now contained among the Apocryphal or Deutero-canonical Books – Susanna, Bel and the Dragon and the Song of the Three Young Men. These in turn have been supplemented by two works from Qumran – the so-called Prayer of Nabonidus which shows striking similarities with the events described in Daniel 4, and a historico-eschatological fragment designated 'Pseudo-Daniel' – and by the Lives of the Prophets dating from the first century AD.

The link-up of the hero of the Book of Daniel, then, with the legendary figure alluded to by Ezekiel and the Aqhat Tale may fall short of 'proof', but there are sufficient indications in the literature of the period to make such an assumption a distinct probability.

2. The book

The Book of Daniel is in two distinct parts: chapters 1–6 contain six stories, five of which have to do with Daniel, told in the third person, i.e. they are anonymous; chapters 7–12 contain four visions, together with their interpretations, and are for the most part described in the first person, i.e. they are pseudonymous. The problems of literary analysis do not concern us here; we simply note that the author of the book, writing between, say 167 BC and 164 BC, in all probability made use of a collection of stories already in existence either in written or, more likely, in oral form and attached to them his account of certain visions which he attributed to the hero of the stories, Daniel the wise man.

The stories themselves are set in the time of the exile in Babylon and tell of the exploits of a Jewish youth, Daniel, with his three companions, and their confrontation with the Babylonian king and his 'wise men' who practise enchantments and idolatry. In each case this confrontation results in a manifestation of the sovereignty of the God of Israel whom even the heathen king is forced to acknowledge. Following the writer's introduction of the Jewish youths (1.1–7), the first story tells of their refusal to take the rich food provided for them at the Babylonian court and of their subsequent vindication, thus demonstrating their loyalty to the food laws of their fathers and the approval of their God (1.8–16) who gives them understanding and wisdom far beyond that of the magicians and wise men in the service of the king (1.17–23).

The second story is about a dream which the king commanded his wise men to recall for him and then to interpret (2.1–11). In desperation they seek out Daniel who, after prayer and praise, is able to describe the dream which concerned a huge image made of four metals and to give its interpretation which concerned four kingdoms: just as the statue in the dream is smashed by a great stone, so the kingdoms will be destroyed by God's everlasting kingdom which will soon be ushered in (2.12–45). The King then recognizes Israel's God as 'God of gods and Lord of lords' (2.46–49).

The third story concerns Daniel's three companions who, on failing to worship the golden image set up by Nebuchadnezzar (3.1–7), are accused (3.8–18) and thrown into a fiery furnace from which they are miraculously delivered (3.19–30).

The fourth story tells of another of the king's dreams – a luxuriant tree which a 'watcher' is commanded to cut down, leaving only its stump in the ground 'bound with a band of iron and bronze'. The one who is represented by the tree will become like one of the brute beasts of the field (4.1–18). Daniel is told to give the interpretation. The king himself is the tree: he will be hewn down, stricken with madness and made to dwell with the wild beasts (4.19–27). This word is fulfilled, but in the end his reason returns and he acknowledges the Most High (4.28 and also 4.1–3).

The fifth story concerns a great feast given by Belshazzar during which he and his princes eat and drink from sacred vessels pillaged from Jerusalem (5.1–4). Suddenly a mysterious hand writes mysterious letters on the wall which no one is able to interpret (5.5–9). Daniel is then summoned and chastizes the king (5.10–23). He proceeds to read and to interpret the writing: 'Mene, mene, teqel and parsin'. God has numbered (*mn'*) Belshazzar's kingdom and is bringing it to an end; he has weighed him (*tql*) and found him wanting, and his kingdom will be divided (*prs*) between the Medes and Persians (5.24–28). Daniel is rewarded by being made third ruler in the kingdom (5.29–31).

The sixth story is set in the reign of Darius the Mede. As a high-ranking officer Daniel has many enemies who plot against him. They persuade the king to issue a decree that no one shall offer prayer to any save the king for the next thirty days. The penalty for disobedience is to be thrown into a den of lions (6.1–9). Daniel is caught in the act and the penalty is carried out (6.10–17). His miraculous deliverance and the destruction of his accusers (6.18–24) force Darius to acknowledge the God of Daniel as 'the living God' (6.25–28).

The four visions purport to have been recieved by Daniel during the exile and 'foretell' by means of signs and symbols the judgment of God on kings and kingdoms soon to arise and the advent of God's eternal kingdom at 'the time of the end'. They in fact reflect the events leading up to the time of writing in the second century BC and the persecution and judgment of Antiochus Epiphanes. Only brief mention need be made here of their contents and meaning.

The first is of four mythological beasts rising from the sea, representing four world-kingdoms: a lion with eagles' wings (Babylon), a bear (Media), a leopard with four wings and four heads (Persia) and a beast with ten horns, 'terrible and dreadful and exceedingly strong' (Alexander the Great and his Seleucid successors) from among which sprouts a little horn with human eyes and a mouth that speaks presumptuously (Antiochus Epiphanes) (7.1–8). There then takes place a theophany during which the beast is slain (7.9–12), and an altogether different kingdom is given to 'one like a son of man', a kingdom that 'shall not be destroyed' (7.13–14). Daniel, with the help of an angel, is given its interpretation and the assurance that 'the saints of the Most High shall receive the kingdom' (7.15–18). These 'saints' will be persecuted by the tenth ('little') horn 'for a time, two times and half a time' (i.e. three and a half years) when his dominion will be taken away and the saints inherit the kingdom (7.19–28).

The second vision is set in 'the reign of Belshazzar' (8.1–2). It shows a ram with two great horns ousted in fight by a he-goat whose great horn is broken in the struggle (8.3–8). But in its place there grow up four horns. Out of one of these sprouts a little horn which exalts itself and takes away the burnt offering in the Temple (8.9–12). This state of affairs is to continue for 2,300 evening and morning (sacrifices), i.e. 1,150 days when the sanctuary will be restored (8.13–14). Gabriel is then bidden to make known to Daniel the interpretation of the vision. It is a vision 'for the time of the end' (8.15–19). The ram with the two horns represents the Medo-Persian kingdom and the shaggy he-goat with the great horn represents the Greek kingdom and Alexander the Great, and the four horns that grow up in its place his successors, the Diadochoi. But attention is focussed on another, full of cunning and deceit, whom the reader recognizes at once as none other than Antiochus himself. His fate is sealed, for 'by no human hand' he will be broken (8.20–25). Daniel is bidden to 'seal up' the vision until the time of the end (8.26–27).

The third revelation comes 'in the first year of Darius' (i.e. 538 BC), not in the form of a dream or vision, but as a result of Daniel's reading the scriptures. In particular, he seeks to know the meaning of Jeremiah's prophecy that the exile would last for seventy years (9.1–2; cf. Jer. 25.11–12; 29.10). After prayer and fasting (9.3–14), Gabriel appears and interprets it to him (9.20–23). The 'seventy years' represent 'seventy weeks of years', i.e. 490 years. These are divided into three unequal parts. The first is a period of seven 'weeks' (i.e. 49 years, presumably from the fall of Jerusalem in 587 BC to 538 BC); the second is for 62 'weeks' (i.e. 434 years, from 538 BC to 170 BC) and one 'week' (i.e. 7 years, from 170 BC to 164 BC), this last being divided into two half 'weeks' (i.e. three-and-a-half years each, from 170 BC to 167 BC and from 167 BC to 164 BC). This first 'week' is to be marked by the desecration of the Temple. After three-and-a-half years the order will be given for 'sacrifice and offering' to cease (This in fact took place in December 167 BC by command of Antiochus). Worse than this will follow: in the place of the altar an appalling 'abomination' will be set up (cf. II Macc. 6.2 which tells how an image of Zeus Olympios, and with it probably a cult symbol, was erected on the holy altar). This state of affairs will continue for three-and-a-half years more, when 'the desolator' will be completely overthrown (9.24–27).

The fourth vision takes the form of an angelic revelation concerning the last days and the historical events leading up to them from the time of the Persian empire onwards. Its description covers the last three chapters of the book, with chapter 10 providing a prologue and chapter 12 an epilogue, chapter 11 containing the vision proper which consists of a long series of cryptic historical events. Daniel is on the bank of the river Tigris when there appears to him a dazzling angelic figure who reveals to him 'a word' which is 'true' and 'a great conflict' (10.1–9). The angel (presumably Gabriel) tells how he had been prevented from coming earlier by the (angelic) 'prince of the kingdom of Persia', until Michael had come to his assistance. When he has carried out his errand he will return to the fight against 'the prince of Persia' and also 'the prince of Greece'. That errand is to let Daniel understand 'what is to befall in the latter days' (10.10–11.1). There then follows the content of 'the word' referred to in 10.1. It is a 'potted' history in which the reader will recognize the escapades of great rulers from Cyrus, through Alexander the Great and his successors, to Antiochus Epiphanes, 'a contemptible person' who will cause many of 'the wise' to fall by the sword (11.2–39). From the stand-point of the author, historical survey now becomes predictive prophecy with its announcement of the speedy arrival of 'the time of the end', for the tyrant 'will come to his end, with none to help him' (11.40–45). But the 'time of trouble' has not yet spent itself: the forces of evil vent their wrath. But Michael comes to the rescue of his people, not only those who are alive at that time, but even those who are dead, for they will rise in resurrection, 'some to everlasting life, and some to shame and everlasting contempt'. Daniel is bidden to 'seal' these 'words' in a book 'until the time of the end' (12.1–4). The scene then changes and Daniel is on the banks of the river Tigris again (cf. 10.4) in the company of two angels. He asks how long it will be before the end comes and is told, 'for a time, two times and half a time'. The books ends with a recalculation of this time-span either by the author himself or, more likely, by a later hand.

3. The additional material

The stories contained in Daniel 1–6 are only part of a larger collection which circulated, first in oral and then in written form, concerning Daniel and his three companions. Although not included in that book (because they did not suit the purpose of the author or else belonged to a somewhat later date), they continued to be prized, not least in Jewish circles in Egypt and came to be included in the old Greek versions. They appear in the Apocrypha as 'Additions' to the Book of Daniel, but in Roman Catholic usage are integral to it.

The first addition is a story about a Jewish matron named Susanna who is falsely accused by two elders of adultery because she had refused to submit to them (vv. 15–27). They make a charge against her and she is sentenced to death (vv. 28–41). But just in time the young lad Daniel comes to her rescue. He challenges the verdict and, questioning the elders separately on the 'evidence', receives different answers from them. The result is that they are stoned to death and Susanna is set free (vv. 42–64).

The second addition consists of two stories. In the first of these (vv. 1–22) the king tries to persuade Daniel of the reality of the god Bel by pointing out how much food he eats each day. Daniel refuses to accept such 'evidence', and so the priests arrange a demonstration. They set the food-offerings in order and close the Temple door which the king seals with his own signet (vv. 1–13). They are confident of the outcome because they have a secret door through which they and their families can enter the Temple and consume the food. But Daniel too is confident and, unbeknown to the priests, he spreads ashes on the Temple floor (vv. 12–15). Next morning the food has gone, but the footprints on the ashes tell their own tale. The guilty are slain and the Temple destroyed (vv. 16–22).

In the second story the king confronts Daniel with the claim that a large dragon, worshipped by the Babylonians, is in truth a living god and bids him worship it also. To prove that this is not so and that his God is the living God Daniel claims to be able to kill the dragon 'without sword or stick' (vv. 23–26). He thereupon makes cakes of pitch, fat and hair which, when swallowed, cause the dragon to burst open and die. The king is favourably impressed, but when his subjects charge him that he has become a Jew, he allows Daniel to be thrown into a lions' den. The lions are ravenous, but for six whole days Daniel sits among them unscathed (vv. 27–32). On the sixth day an angel brings the prophet Habakkuk to him who provides him with food (vv. 33–39). Next day the king finds Daniel unharmed. Daniel's accusers are made to take his place and are immediately devoured (vv. 40–42).

Whereas the first and second additions are placed at the end of the canonical Book of Daniel as extra chapters, the third is to be read between 3.23 and 3.24 and tells how Shadrach, Meshach and Abednego are thrown into a burning fiery furnace. It consists, in the main, of two liturgical compositions in verse, the prayer of Azariah (Abednego) (vv. 3–22) and the Song of the Three Young Men (vv. 29–68), introduced (vv. 1–2) and joined together (vv. 23–28) by passages in prose. In Azariah's prayer he confesses the sin of the nation: the people have broken the covenant and can do nothing to set things right. He offers repentance and pleads for deliverance that their enemies may come to acknowledge the sovereignty of 'the only God' (vv. 3–22).

Their opponents, however, keep feeding the flames which leap to a height of forty-nine cubits and burn them to death. But the angel of the Lord stands beside the three young men and makes 'a moist whistling wind' in the midst of the furnace so that the fire does not touch them (vv. 23–27). They then join in a hymn of praise to God (vv. 29–68), calling on all creation to unite with them and summoning Israel to exalt him for ever. They themselves will continue to bless him whose 'mercy endures for ever'.

Further confirmation of a cycle of material supplementary to that of the Book of Daniel itself is provided by several fragments of two works written in Aramaic found among the Dead Sea scrolls. The first is the so-called Prayer of Nabonidus, the last king of the Babylonians. It tells how he had been smitten 'with a malignant disease' for seven years whilst in Teima where he worshipped gods 'of silver, gold, (bronze, iron,) wood, stone and clay'. But, on confessing his faults, he was cured by 'an exorcist . . . a Jew from among the (children of the exile of Judah)'. This has a close resemblance to Nebuchadnezzar's miraculous recovery referred to in Daniel 4. Indeed it may suggest that the name of Nabonidus and not that of Nebuchadnezzar appeared in the original tradition contained in this chapter. The document itself is later than the biblical book, but it may well reflect an earlier form of the story recorded there.

The second work is usually designated 'Pseudo-Daniel'. It refers to one called 'son of God' and 'son of the Most High', a figure to be distinguished apparently from 'the people of God'. When the time comes for him to arise, all conflict will cease. The significance of the titles given to him is not too clear, but they are not obviously messianic (cf. G. Vermes, *The Dead Sea Scrolls: Qumran in Perspective*, ²1982, pp. 73f.).

An interesting account of Daniel, with accompanying embellishments, is given in the Lives of the Prophets (first century AD) which describes him as a member of the royal family (4.1; cf. *Ant.* X.186), a chaste and holy man, gaunt in appearance but 'beautiful in the favour of the Most High' (4.3). During Nebuchadnezzar's period of madness, when he ate grass 'like an ox' and 'forgot that he had been a man', Daniel prayed for him incessantly. Nebuchadnezzar was indeed a pitiful sight, for 'his eyes were like raw flesh from weeping' (4.10); but Daniel's prayers were effective – the king repented, his period of trial was reduced from seven years to seven months and he was restored to the throne (4.13). Thereafter 'he wrought many prodigies for other kings of the Persians which they did not write down' and, having given a warning portent concerning the coming fate of Babylon, our hero died and was buried with great honour in the royal grotto (4.18ff.).

4. The man

The Book of Daniel is essentially 'a tract for the times': the qualities of the man Daniel reflect those very qualities most highly prized in the community from which the author came and indicate the concerns prevalent at that time.

(a) A man of courage

Thus, again and again he is shown as a man of great courage and fortitude whose trust in God keeps him safe from man and beast and so serves as an encouragement for others. So too in the extra-biblical literature where the legendary element is heightened as when the furnace flames leapt forty-nine cubits high (The Song of the Three Young Men v. 24) or the seven lions are given 'two human bodies and two sheep' every day to satisfy their hunger but leave Daniel unscathed (Bel and the Dragon v. 32).

His courage, however, is more than physical. It is a spiritual quality which finds expression, for example, in abstinence from certain foods and drinks (Dan. 1.8ff.) – a point which would not be lost on the readers of the book for whom dietry laws and other such regulations were of supreme importance. Stress is laid, too, on the place Daniel gives to prayer, even when its practice may involve him in great risk (cf. 6.11ff). In the Lives of the Prophets he is introduced as 'a holy man' (4.16) whose prayer for the king reduces his period of madness from seven years to seven months (4. 12–13). His resolute opposition to idolatry is also emphasized, be it in the form of a graven image or a craven king, an all-too-relevant matter to the reader who would readily recall Antiochus's self-designation 'Epiphanes', 'God manifest'. The same theme is further pursued in the Additions where Daniel exposes the chicaneries of the worshippers of Bel and destroys the Beast that has the arrogance to claim divine authority. He serves 'the living God' who alone controls kings and nations. His courage and faithfulness bring their own reward and the pledge of divine protection. Indeed, he comes to be honoured by men as well as by God: Nebuchadnezzar offers him the same name and status as his own son (Lives of the Prophets 4.15) and, at the end of his days, he is buried 'with great honour in the royal grotto' (4.18).

(b) A man of wisdom

Writing about the Book of Daniel, E. W. Heaton comments that 'in our own day, its author would certainly have been a Doctor of Divinity and would, in all probability, have occupied a Professorial Chair of Biblical Exegesis' (op. cit., p. 19). He was certainly an able man and counted himself among 'the wise' (cf. Dan. 11.33) who found their delight in 'the Law of the Lord'. The man Daniel of whom he writes typifies this same outlook, for he too is presented as a 'wise man' whose wisdom far surpasses that of the Babylonian sages.

These sages are introduced as 'the Chaldeans' (1.4), a term which initially referred to the dynasty founded in Babylon by Nebuchadnezzar's father, but in subsequent writings came to indicate a class of influential Babylonian priests with a reputation for learning in astrology, divination and the magical arts. In the Book of Daniel they are introduced as soothsayers, sorcerers, magicians and enchanters. The story of Daniel is told to show, beyond a peradventure, that this Babylonian wisdom cannot begin to compare with that wisdom given by God to his own people Israel.

This is abundantly demonstrated when the king bids Daniel recall for him a dream which his 'wise men' cannot identify, and to give its interpretation (ch. 2). The account that follows reminds the reader clearly of the story of Joseph in Genesis 41 and his part in interpreting Pharaoh's dream of seven years' famine and seven years' plenty. In both stories the hero is promoted to become head of state and chief of the sages (cf. 2.48 and Gen. 41. 40ff.). The Chaldean soothsayers and magicians may consult their sacred books of predictions and incantations, but their efforts will be of no avail. They are unable to tell the present, far less the future!

The divine wisdom, then, given to Daniel is altogether different from the magical enchantments and prognostications of 'the Chaldeans' with their secret learning and accumulated esoteric lore. He too can interpret dreams and foretell the future and cure diseases; but the wisdom that makes this possible is God-given and God-inspired and consists of a spiritual insight into the mind and purpose of God which sees meaning in mysteries and the hand of God in the affairs of men.

Such wisdom makes two things plain. One is that the whole of history is a unity and is in the control of God despite all the signs to the contrary. The world-powers of Babylonia, Media, Persia and Greece rise only to fall. They are given their allotted span and will cease to be. Nothing can be more sure than this, for God has allotted to them their number of years and has determined when their time is up. History is systematically arranged and divinely determined. Men cannot alter what God has laid down: but by means of divine wisdom they can discover at what point they now stand and so be in a position to predict what is yet to be.

This points to the second emphasis made plain by divine wisdom: the kingdoms of this world are soon to give way to the irresistible power of God's coming kingdom, for the end is at hand! The stone 'cut out without hands' will smash in pieces the great image (2.31ff.). The four great beasts (7.1ff.) will be destroyed and 'dominion and glory and a kingdom' will be given to 'one like a son of man', none other than 'the saints of the Most High' (7.18). But first there will be a time of great tribulation. During that time, Michael, the patron angel of Israel, will deliver them and they will inherit the kingdom here on this earth. That kingdom they will share eternally with the illustrious dead who will be raised in resurrection to participate in it. Evil will be destroyed and the wicked will rise to share only in shame and everlasting contempt (12.1ff.).

(c) A man of vision

Such pronouncements and predictions are generally made as a result of Daniel's ability to understand and interpret dreams and visions.

Sometimes they are his own, at other times they are the king's. In either case they are God's chosen vehicle of revelation.

Like Enoch, he sometimes finds himself in the Heavenly Council in the company of an angelic interpreter (cf. 7.15f.). But, unlike Enoch, he is not taken on flights to the heavens or to the extremities of the earth. The emphasis rather is that of prediction through the interpretation of dreams. By this means he is able to disclose those 'mysteries' which have been revealed to him concerning the course of history and its fulfilment in God's kingdom. If divine wisdom is the inspiration of such disclosure, the dream is its vehicle of operation: 'There is a God in heaven who reveals mysteries . . . Not because of any wisdom that I have more than all the living has this mystery been revealed to me, but in order that the interpretation may be made known to the king' (2.28,30).

But although Daniel does not record visits to the heavenly realms, he is every bit as conscious as Enoch was of the inter-relationship between heaven and earth and of the part played in the world's affairs by the angelic hosts. This is highlighted in Daniel 10, where, as we have seen, Michael the patron archangel of Israel enters into battle with the patron archangels of Persia and of Greece. Such angels and archangels are, as it were, a heavenly counterpart of the Gentile rulers into whose hands God has, from time to time, delivered his people. The events in heaven correspond to or even determine events on earth. An angel's ascendancy over his peers in the heavens results in the ascendancy of the nation it represents over its foes, and correspondingly in the case of their defeat. The key to earthly history is to be found in heavenly event. History takes on a supramundane character so that its ultimate meaning is to be found in the realm of spiritual being.

It is probably within this kind of setting that we have to understand the reference in Daniel 7 to 'one like a son of man' (7.13) who, a few verses later, seems to be identified with 'the saints of the Most High' (7.18). Here, the 'son of man' (i.e. a human figure representing an angel, as distinct from the four beasts representing the nations) is probably to be taken as the heavenly counterpart of the Jewish people. His authority is their authority, his rule is their rule, his kingdom is their kingdom.

The figure of Daniel thus presented in this cycle of tradition, and pre-eminently in the book that bears his name, is shaped by the character of the times in which the writers lived and by the form of presentation in story, dream and vision. From an obscure past he emerges as a great hero and exemplar to the whole nation.

V

Job, the Patient Sufferer

1. The legend

The biblical wisdom literature, of which the Book of Job forms an important part, is to be understood against an international background and reflects the moral and religious teaching of cultures other than that of the Hebrew people. In particular, the problem of suffering is the subject of a number of literary works in Egypt and Mesopotamia dating from as far back as the second millennium BC. One example of this is an Egyptian writing entitled, 'The dispute of the soul of one who is tired of life'. The dispute in question is as to whether the sufferer, tired of living, should find a way out of his misery by committing suicide. It contains some distinct resemblances to the plight of the biblical Job and its contrast with his former prosperity, and emphasizes his longing for death. Again, in 'The Tale of the Eloquent Peasant', whose pleas for justice receive their due reward, there is a similarity even in literary form, with its prose prologue and epilogue as in the Book of Job itself.

Among the Babylonian sources, perhaps the best-known parallel is the so-called 'Babylonian Job' which tells how the hero of the story is stricken with illness and misfortune despite the fact that he has with the utmost care carried out his duties towards the gods. But the gods remain silent and inscrutable, and in despair he cries, 'Who can understand the counsel of the gods?' The parallels here to the Book of Job are recognizable even to the point of a number of details; but even where there are no such indications and no direct dependence on earlier stories and legends, their common concern and expression indicate a common reservoir from which they draw.

None of these sources is associated with a man called Job; but it is of interest to observe that this name (Hebrew, *'yyob*) is to be found, with variations, in both Egyptian and Akkadian texts belonging to the second millennium BC. M. H. Pope, after examining a number of these sources, comments: 'The authenticity and antiquity of the name *'Ayyab>'Iyyob* is thus well attested . . . It is an ordinary name and may have been chosen for this reason, or it may be that some ancient worthy bearing it actually experienced a fate such as described in the biblical story and became the type and model of the righteous sufferer' (*The Interpreter's Dictionary of the Bible*, vol. 2, p. 911). The Book of Job as it stands is a post-exilic work, but there is reason to believe that the prose narratives are of an earlier date and contain reflections of an old Job legend within the traditions of the Hebrew people. Hence the references, alluded to more than once already, in Ezekiel 14.14,20 where Job is set alongside two other heroes of antiquity, Noah and Daniel, who together are praised for their righteousness before God.

Whatever the origins of the Job legend may have been, its continuation in the post-biblical period, as we shall see, retained, if not memories, then associations with the ancient past and identified Job with the patriarchs of old.

2. The literature

During the period 200 BC-AD 200 the Job legend finds varied expression in a number of writings which give added information concerning his ancestry and the members of his immediate family. In three of these Job is identified with Jobab who, according to Genesis 36.33, succeeded Bela, the first king of Edom.

The first of these sources is the Septuagint Addition to Job which states that 'Jobab, called Job' was the second king of Edom (42.17d; cf. Gen. 36.33) and the grandson of Esau, fifth in line from Abraham (42.17c); Job's friends are also identified as royal personages – Eliphaz of the sons of Esau is the king of Taiman, Baldad is the ruler of the Sauchites, and Sophar is the king of the Minneans (42.17e)

The second source is Aristeas the Exegete (before the first century BC) where it is stated that 'Job was formerly called Jobab' (*Praeparatio Evangelica* 9.25.3) as the text stands, he is said to be the *son* of Esau, but this should in all probability be *grandson* (there would appear to be some confusion in the text arising from haplography) in keeping with the evidence of the other two sources; the added information is given that he 'dwelt in Ausitis on the borders of Idumea and Arabia' in the patriarchal age (*Praeparatio Evangelica* 9.25.1; cf. also Septuagint Addition).

The third source is the Testament of Job (first century BC – first century AD), the full title of which is, 'The book of the words of Job, the one called Jobab' who is 'of the sons of Esau' (1.6). Here the reason for his change of name is given: 'I used to be Jobab before the Lord called me Job. When I was called Jobab I lived quite near a venerated idol's temple . . . I began reasoning within myself saying, "Is this really the God who made heaven and earth?" ' In other words, his change of name is a mark of his change of allegiance. Further information is also given about his family: his first wife is called Sitis and his second wife Dinah, the daughter of Jacob (1.6; 25.1; cf. Pseudo-Philo 8.8). We note that in the biblical Job the first of these is not named and the second is not mentioned.

The Testament of Job is the most significant of these three sources. It may have originated among the Jewish sect that goes by the name 'Therapeutae', but in any case is a Jewish work with, perhaps, some degree of Christian influence. Its form is that of a 'testament', fairly common at the time of writing, in which the aged Job, on the point of death, addresses his 'seven sons and three daughters' (1.2) with words of wisdom. It contains more *haggadic* material than the general run of testaments of the period, dressing up the story with embellishments in the form of 'frills' and legends not found in the biblical account. Its purpose is to give encouragement to its readers by telling stories of Job's amazing patience and endurance in face of great pain and provocation. The indications are that it was written in Egypt and illustrates, in its expressed beliefs and customs, how rich and varied was the piety of the hellenized Jewry of that time.

Having summoned his ten children by Dinah, he recalls that his former wife had died bitterly along with their ten other children and commends to them his own patient endurance (1.2–6; cf. Jas. 5.11). He tells them of his conversion from idolatry and his change of name from Jobab to Job. An angel then appears to him in a vision and gives him permission to purge the idolatrous temple nearby (3.1–7). It is the place of Satan, and Job must expect great conflict; but through patient endurance, like an athlete, he will win the crown (4.1–11). And so, with the help of fifty youths, he levels the temple to the ground; he then withdraws to his house and barricades the door (5.1–3)! The struggle with Satan is about to begin.

For twenty-one whole chapters that struggle continues (6.1–27.7).

Satan first comes disguised as a beggar, but is told to depart (6.1–6). He tries again and this time Job gives him a loaf, burnt to a cinder! Satan threatens that he will do to Job's body what Job has done to the loaf (7.1–13). Satan then implores God to give him authority to take away Job's wealth, and this is granted (8.1–3).

That wealth is now described, together with Job's benevolence, munificence and lavish charity. From his many thousands of sheep, camels and she-asses he had a standing order in favour of the orphans and widows, the poor and needy (9.1–8). His lavish hospitality towards the poor kept fifty bakeries in full operation (10.1–7). He made loans to help people set up in business so that they in turn could give to the poor (11.1–12). In like manner he willingly paid the workmen their wages (12.1–4). So productive were his cows that 'the mountains were awash with milk and became as congealed butter' (13.1–6). If there were any complaints among the servants, his chanting and his playing the lyre would soothe their hearts (14.1–5). Having thus expressed himself, he offers lavish sacrifices on behalf of his children and bids that the meat left over be given to the poor with the plea that they pray for his children that they may be saved from pride (15.1–9).

Satan now sets to work. First he destroys by fire Job's herds and flocks; some remain, but these are confiscated by men whom Job had treated well. And yet, he refuses to blaspheme God (16.1–7). Then the devil (for so he is called), disguised this time as the king of the Persians, gathers together a gang of rogues, smashes Job's house and kills his children. Job is utterly exhausted, but counts the delights of the heavenly city, to which he is heading, as of greater worth than all his possessions (18.1–8). Despite his dire trouble he blesses the name of the Lord (19.1–4). Having taken his goods and his children, Satan now asks God for Job's body to inflict it with the plague. Permission is granted and, having been knocked from his throne and pinned beneath it for three hours, he is struck with a severe plague so that worms fill his body (20.1–9). For forty-eight years he remains on a dung heap outside the city. From there he sees his first wife Sitis working as a slave to get him bread to eat (21.1–4). When restrictions are placed on its supply, Satan dresses himself as a bread-seller from whom Sitis begs bread, thinking him to be a man. In lieu of money he asks for the hair of her head which he then shears off (22.1–23.11). She bewails her lot and mocks her husband and his hope of salvation (24.1–10). The lament that follows highlights even further the depths to which Sitis has fallen (25.1–8). Let Job speak some word against the Lord and die and by so doing relieve her of her weariness and weakness of heart (25.9–10). Job finds his wife's words most depressing, but reminds her of all the good they have received at God's hands and pleads for patience. Can't she see that Satan is standing behind her, unsettling her reason and trying to deceive them both (26.1–6)? And so he challenges Satan outright to come out and fight! Satan weeps and acknowledges defeat. Like a wrestler he had pinned Job down and filled his mouth with sand; but Job had got the better of him in the end, and Satan left him alone for three years. Let Job's children be patient, 'for patience is better than everything' (27.1–7).

Following this confrontation with Satan, there now takes place a dialogue with Job's 'friends', here introduced as 'kings': Elious (= Elihu), Eliphas, Baldas, and Sophar in that order (it may be that 'Elious' should read 'Eliphas' at 31.1–5 and 32.1 which would then give the sequence found in the biblical book). The kings, then, arrive to comfort Job, 'the king of all Egypt', who has by now been suffering for twenty years. So bad is his plight that they and others fail to recognize him. For seven whole days they sit in silence before him as he contemplates his lot (28.1–9). On being assured that he is 'Jobab', their 'fellow king', they collapse as if dead (29.1–30.5). After seven days the kings decide to 'check him out' and go to see him again. But so great is the stench that they have to douse the place with incense (31.1–4). Job's identity having been confirmed, Eliphas offers a lament with the repeated refrain, 'Where, then, is the splendour of your throne?' (32.1–11). Job replies that his throne is in heaven and his kingdom is for ever and ever (33.1–9). Eliphas, in disgust, threatens to leave and return home. Baldas restrains him and suggests they ought to check whether or not Job may be mentally deranged (35.1–6). In reply to further interrogation Job asserts his belief in the stability of heaven (36.1–6). Questions and counter-questions follow and Job declares, 'My mind is sound' (37.1–38.5). Sophar now speaks up and grants that Job's intelligence is unaffected, but shows his doubt by offering the services of their three physicians. Job declines: his healing is from the Lord who created the physicians (38.6–8).

Just then Sitis his wife arrives in rags. She begs the kings to recover the bones of her children from the ruins of their shattered house for proper burial. But Job forbids them: the children have already been taken up to heaven. The kings think him mad (39.1–13), but just then they, with Job and Sitis, see a vision of the children 'crowned with the splendour of the heavenly one'. For Sitis this is their true memorial.

She rises and returns to her city where she dies. Even the dumb animals weep over her (40.1–14).

Elious now speaks up, inspired by Satan, and insults Job, stating that his claims of a throne in heaven are just imaginery (41.1–6). God himself now intervenes and censures Elious and shows himself in healing to Job 'through a hurricane and clouds'. At God's command he offers sacrifice for Eliphas and his two friends that their sin may be forgiven (42.1–8), but not for Elious who is considered unworthy and a representative of 'the evil one'. Eliphas recites an imprecatory hymn condemning Elious in strong language (43.1–17). Job then returns to his own city; God prospers his estate and he begins again to help the poor (44.1–5). But he realizes his time has come to die, and so he counsels his children to do good to the poor (45.1–4).

He then distributes his possessions among his seven sons. The three daughters express disappointment, but Job has reserved for them a better inheritance still. To each he gives a multi-coloured sash, shimmering with heavenly glory (46.1–9). These (magical) sashes will cause them to experience a better world than any they have known. He had proved it himself, for through their power he had been cured of his plague. They are in fact protective amulets from God the Father; they will help them see beyond the seen to the unseen (47.1–11). One after another the daughters put the sashes on and immediately they 'spoke ecstatically in the angelic dialect', no longer caring for earthly things but glorifying God (48.1–50.3). Nereus, brother of Job, in the presence of Job and the holy angel who has appeared earlier on, writes down the daughters' hymns of praise and preserves them in a book (51.1–4). After three days Job falls ill though, on account of the sash he wore, he feels no pain. As his daughters praise God he sees 'the gleaming chariots which had come for his soul'. The one who 'sits in the great chariot' takes his soul and sets off for the east and his body is carried to the tomb (52.1–12). And so amid weeping and lamenting he who has 'received a name renowned in all generations for ever' is laid to rest 'in a beautiful sleep' (53.1–8).

3. The man

In the Testament of Abraham (see chapter 6), which probably belongs to the same time and place as the Testament of Job, it is said: 'There is no man like unto him (Abraham) on earth, not even Job, the wondrous man' (15.15). The same kind of language is used in the

Testament of Job itself at the time of his burial: 'He received a name renowned in all generations for ever' (53.8). Descended from Esau and Abraham and married to Jacob's daughter, he stood in a great line of succession. But, apart from that, he lived an altogether exemplary life in spite of many trials and provocations. The biblical Book of Job provides the basic elements out of which the figure in the Testament and corresponding sources is to develop. But considerable changes take place that advance his reputation and standing in the traditions of early Judaism.

(a) His kingly status

Already in the Septuagint, as we have seen, Job's friends are described as 'kings'. So too in the Testament of Job and the other sources mentioned above. The Testament goes further and introduces Job himself as a king (31.15), more precisely as 'the king of all Egypt' (28.7) whose territory he will not allow Satan to conquer (33.7). He sits on his throne (20.4) and men are dazzled by its glorious splendour (32.2–12). It is easy to see the seeds from which such a tradition grew, for in the Book of Job itself, Job likens himself to 'a king among his troops' (Job 29.25) and elsewhere complains that God has 'taken the crown from my head' (19.9; cf. 31.36). Hints given there now become facts and Job assumes royal status.

(b) His wealth

Here again the starting point is the canonical Book of Job which describes Job's wealth in cattle and sheep and many other possessions (Job 1.3; 42.10ff.). But now tradition attempts to 'garnish the lily' by detailing in fulsome and extravagant terms his fabulous wealth: 130,000 sheep (with eighty dogs to guard them), 9,000 camels, 3,000 yoke of oxen and 140,000 she-asses, not to mention his great house with its servants and two hundred watch-dogs to guard it (9.1–10.7)! So great is the yield from his cows that the dairy-maids grow weary, milk flows everywhere and butter piles up into butter-mountains (13.1–3). His meat-cuts are sought after (13.6) as is the bread from his fifty bakeries (10.7) The measure of his wealth can be gauged by the lavishness of the sacrifices he offers on behalf of each of his ten children: three-hundred doves, fifty goats' kids and twelve sheep (13.4f.). Yet in all this he resists pride (15.8). Not only is he rich, he is also righteous (41.3). All these are taken from him, including his wife and children. But when at last he is healed of his plague he is given another wife and another ten children (1.2ff.). The Lord blesses all his goods and doubles his estate (44.5).

(c) His deeds of charity

Job's fabulous wealth is matched only by his lavish generosity. He ordered 7,000 sheep to be sheared for clothing to be given to 'orphans and widows, the poor and the helpless'; 3,000 camels were used in the distribution of goods to the destitute, and there was a standing agreement for the offspring of five-hundred she-asses to be sold and given to the poor (9.1–6). In his own house there were thirty tables always spread and available, marked 'for strangers only', and another twelve for widows. He loaned out his oxen on free-hire so that people could plough their fields; he allotted produce for the poor and put his fifty bakeries at their disposal. He sent no one empty away (10.1–7). Others he set up in business by providing the necessary capital, 'taking no security from them except a written note'. Sometimes such people prospered; sometimes they were robbed. In that case he would cancel their debt (11.8–12) and rejoice that they had taken the money in the first place (11.5). He would press his workmen to take their wages so as to help them in their cheerful task of giving to the poor (12.1–4). In such generosity he set an example to others (44.4), not least to his own children whom he counselled before he died: 'Do not forget the Lord. Do good to the poor. Do not overlook the helpless' (45.1–3). This was true piety and real religion.

(d) His victory over Satan

Job, when he was still called Jobab, lived near a heathen temple where sacrifices and libations were offered. There came a time when he began to question the worship offered there, and the angel revealed to him that it was indeed 'the place of Satan'. Job is determined to purge the place and to destroy it. The angel warns him of the dire consequences of any such action, for Satan will fight against him; but in the end Job will be raised up and restored. He accordingly razes the temple to the ground, returns home and barricades the door, ready for battle (2.1–5.3). The story of the burnt loaf carries its own dire warning of trouble ahead for Job (7.1ff.); but already he has shown great wisdom and penetrating insight in seeing through Satan's disguise as a beggar (6.4) and will do so again when he comes as a seller of bread (23.1ff.). But Satan wreaks his vengeance, having been given authority by God so to do (8.1–3). Job loses almost everything he possesses – livestock, children, house, health and wife (16.1–26. 6; 40.1–14). But in the end he challenges Satan with the utmost confidence: 'Come up front! Stop hiding yourself! Does a lion show his strength in a cage? Does a fledgling take flight when it is in a basket? Come out and fight' (27.1)! Satan is routed and retires in tears (27.6f.). Later on, Job's powers of insight allow him to see Satan at work again, this time in the person of Elious, 'the evil one' (43.5), who speaks under his influence and inspiration (41.5). The victory is won.

(e) His patient endurance

One big difference between the biblical Book of Job and these other sources at our disposal is that, in the latter, little or nothing is said about the questioning and complaining of Job concerning the injustice of his suffering; the whole emphasis is now laid on his patience and endurance which know no limit. Written perhaps at a time of difficulty or even persecution, the Testament of Job, for example, is also 'a tract for the times', encouraging the people to emulate God's servant Job who suffered greatly but endured to the end.

The Testament begins with Job introducing himself as a man 'fully engaged in endurance' (1.5), affirming that he will remain so until he dies (5.1). The angel assures him in God's name that, if he is patient, his name will be renowned in all generations for ever (4.6). He shows this quality in his business transactions (11.10), but above all in his reaction to his own physical suffering. Satan had taken his goods, but was unable to provoke him to contempt (20.1). And now that his body was full of discharges and riddled with worms (20.7ff.) he would continue to endure. Indeed, if a worm were to find its way out, he would replace it where it had been until it was directed otherwise by God who ordained its task (20.8ff.). At the beginning he had been warned that he would be like 'a sparring athlete' and would have to suffer much pain before winning the crown (4.10). This indeed was how it turned out to be because, in his conflict with Satan, he was 'in deep distress'. Like a wrestler he had been pressed to the floor, choking with sand and bruised in every limb, but he showed great endurance and won in the end. In the same way his children must show patient endurance in everything that happens to them (27.1–7). So too must his wife Sitis, for if we have received good from God's hand, should we not in turn endure evil (26.4)?

(f) His witness to heavenly realities

In the Testament of Job there are no visits to the heavenly places in company with an angelic interpreter. Nevertheless, there is a deep awareness on the part of Job of the reality of that other realm where God dwells with 'the holy ones' over against the transcience of life here on earth.

This is brought out clearly in a telling parable. Job likens himself to a man wishing to enter a certain city to share in its wealth and splendour. To this end he embarks on a ship which runs into a violent storm. So great is his desire to reach the city that he is willing to throw his precious cargo into the sea, for, says he, 'I considered my goods as nothing compared to the city about which the angel spoke to me' (18.6–8). That heavenly city to which he will be raised in resurrection (4.9) is the place where his throne is. His earthly throne may be overturned (20.5) and he himself may be in great distress (20.7), but his true throne is 'in the upper world'; its splendour and majesty come from the right hand of the Father (33.3) and his kingdom is for ever and ever (33.9). This world will pass away (33.4), for 'the earth and those who dwell in it are unstable' (36.3), but 'there is no upset in heaven'. For this reason his heart is not fixed on earthly concerns, but on heavenly (36.3f). That hope which he has for himself is already a reality for his children who had so cruelly died, for they are now crowned with the splendour of heaven (40.3).

The reality of heaven and its wonders is brought out even more vividly in the account of the magical sashes given by Job to his daughters. These have heavenly properties and the wearing of them will ensure that all will go well with them (46.7–9). More than that, they will 'lead them into a better world, to live in the heavens' (47.3). Not only had they healed Job of the plagues, 'they spoke to me', he said, 'in power, showing me things present and things to come' (47.6–9). As soon as the daughters put them on they were 'no longer minded toward earthly things', but spoke in the angelic language of heaven (48.1–3).

The Testament ends with Job's death and burial. Just before he died, however, he saw 'the gleaming chariots' coming for his soul (52.6). Unlike Enoch and Elijah, it was Job's soul that was taken, whilst his body was buried in a tomb, no doubt to await the resurrection (55.7).

Job thus becomes a hero figure for the Jewish people living in troublesome days. No matter what might happen to him by way of suffering and loss, he is the great exemplar of patient endurance for whom the glories of heaven are more real and lasting than the glories of earth. His reward is assured – in his children after him who inherit his gifts and in the certainty of life everlasting.

VI

The Three Patriarchs:
Abraham, Isaac and Jacob

1. The sources

The three patriarchs – Abraham, Isaac and Jacob – were not only the forebears of the people of Israel, they were at the same time guarantors of that special relationship which existed between God and his 'covenant people'. Because God had entered into covenant with them, he would continue to do good to their children (II Macc. 1.2) and as he had put the patriarchs to the test, so he would do also to his covenant people (Judith 8.26). As such they were held in high honour by the Jews and it is not surprising that, in course of time, they should become the object of considerable speculation and that imaginative and legendary material should gather round them, some of it an extension of the biblical record and some of it having rather tenuous connections, if any at all. Thus, it was believed in some quarters that they were without sin (Prayer of Manasseh 8) or that they had been formed before the creation of the world (Prayer of Joseph, Fragment A, 1–2).

First in time of appearance (before the first century BC) are two fragments relating to Abraham preserved in Eusebius's *Praeparatio Evangelica* 9.17.2–9 and 9.18.2 and quoting the historian Alexander Polyhistor. The first of these has generally been assigned to a 'Pseudo-Eupolemus' (for the writings of Eupolemus see p. 96) whom many scholars believe to have been an unidentified Samaritan author. The second fragment is anonymous and probably reflects a collection of traditions concerning Abraham's ancestry brought together by Alexander Polyhistor.

Further information concerning Abraham is given in a wide range of books covering several centuries. In the Book of Jubilees (second century BC), for example, a lengthy account is given of the lives of the patriarchs which is both selective and speculative (cf. 11.9 – 46.10) and is made to serve the purpose the author has in mind in writing this book. The treatment is more brief in Pseudo-Philo's Book of Biblical Antiquities (first century AD), but here again extra-biblical material of a legendary kind finds expression (cf. 6–8).

The Apocalypse of Abraham (late first century or second century AD) is of a different literary kind. Conscious of Israel's calling as God's covenant people, it condemns idolatry (cf. 1–8) and then goes on to describe a revelation given to Abraham in seven visions which concludes with God's condemnation of the wicked and his vindication of the righteous in typically apocalyptic style. The so-called Testament of Abraham (first to second century AD) is closely related to two other writings, all of which seem to be deeply influenced by Christian editing and were certainly popular in Christian circles. These are the Testament of Isaac (second century AD) and the Testament of Jacob (second to third century AD?) which may well have derived from the Testament of Abraham. Thus the death of Abraham, which is a prominent feature of the Testament of that name, is referred to in each of the other two which record also the deaths of Isaac and Jacob.

Further information concerning Jacob is given in three other writings of the same or later periods: the Ladder of Jacob (first century AD), the Prayer of Joseph (first century AD) and the Prayer of Jacob (first to fourth century AD). The first of these, in a confused text, is a commentary on Jacob's dream in Genesis 28.11–22 and contains an apocalyptic vision of the future. The second concerns the rivalry of the angels Israel and Uriel over their respective ranks in heaven: and the third consists of invocations and petitions and has, like the second of these books, a certain affinity with Jewish magical texts of the third century AD. In all three, interesting comments are made concerning the patriarchs which highlight still further the speculative element in writings of this kind.

2. Abraham

(a) A legendary hero

Among the pseudepigraphical writings the Book of Jubilees makes ample use of *haggadic* material, i.e. exegesis or explanation in the form of anecdote, to describe the biblical story on which it is based. Thus, in 11.9ff. it elaborates on the words of Genesis 15.11 which tells how Abraham prepared a sacrifice 'and when birds of prey came down upon the carcasses, Abram drove them away'. In Jubilees the predators become 'crows and birds', sent by none other than Mastema the prince of demons, which consume the seed from the field and the fruit from the trees so that there is great hardship. At the time of the next sowing Abraham, a lad of fourteen years old, used to run out and scare the crows away so that not one settled on the fields. This he did seventy times, 'and his reputation was great in all the land of Chaldea'.

This mention of farming leads the writer on to tell how Abraham taught the Chaldeans agriculture (11.23ff.) and what we might call agricultural technology. Not only did he teach the skilled carpenter to make farm implements, he also invented a plough-attachment allowing the seed to drop from a container on the plough-handle through a tube and into the ground at the back of the blade so that the birds were unable to see it!

The reference in 12.14 to the death of Haran by fire in Ur of the Chaldees is also of interest in that it recalls a somewhat similar legend in later Jewish literature involving Abraham who was rescued from a fiery furnace into which he had been cast for refusing to take part in idolatrous practice. Both legends may well have arisen from a literal interpretation of Genesis 15.7: 'I am the Lord who brought you from Ur of the Chaldeans' where, as we have already noted, the word 'ur' means 'flame' or 'fire'. The story, as it concerns Abraham, is well told, for example, in Pseudo-Philo's Book of Biblical Antiquities 6.1ff. There it is associated with the building of the Tower of Babel. The people are bidden to bake bricks in the fire. All do so except twelve men, Abraham among them. For so doing they are threatened with death by burning. But having been given seven days respite in which to repent, they are given the opportunity to escape from prison. Abraham alone refuses, saying, 'I will not be moved from my place where they have put me'. And so he is thrown into the fiery furnace 'along with the bricks'. 'But God caused a great earthquake, and the fire gushing out of the furnace leaped forth in flames and sparks of flame. And it burned all those standing around in sight of the furnace. And all those who were burned in that day were 83,500. And there was not the least injury to Abram from the burning of the fire' (Book of Bibl. Ant. 6.17).

In the same chapter of Jubilees, Abraham is presented in a different light, this time as an observer of the stars (12.16ff.). The inspiration for this no doubt comes from Genesis 15.5 where God says to him, 'Look toward heaven, and number the stars, if you are able to number them'. In the Jubilees passage he is portrayed as observing from evening till daybreak the signs of the stars, the sun and the moon to see what they have to tell concerning the coming of rain. We are reminded in this connection of the Jewish astrological document, The Treatise of Shem (first century BC) which states: 'And if the year begins in Leo, there will be spring rains, then the soil will be deprived of the north winds' (5.1). In the Jubilees passage, however, Abraham comes to realize that such things are not determined by any zodiacal signs, but are in the hands of 'the living God' who hears and answers prayers for rain. This condemnation of astrology is in keeping with the attitude adopted by I Enoch 8.3 which states that it is evil, having been taught by one of the fallen angels, and with the judgment expressed in the Sibylline Oracles (second century BC) which dismisses the practice of astronomy and astrological predictions as 'erroneous, such as foolish men inquire into day by day' (3.218ff.).

On the other hand, the Jewish writer Artapanus (third to second century BC) states that Abraham taught astrology to the Egyptian king (*Praeparatio Evangelica* 9.18.1), and Pseudo-Eupolemus (before first century BC) records that Abraham, having obtained knowledge of astrology in Babylonia, passed it on to the Phoenicians and then to the Egyptians (9.17.3,4,8; cf. *Ant.* I.156,168). This latter reference begins with an account of the scattering of the giants who had built the Tower of Babel and goes on to state that Abraham, born in a Babylonian city, obtained there 'the knowledge of astrology and the Chaldean craft' and 'excelled all in nobility and wisdom . . . and pleased God because he eagerly sought to be reverent' (9.17.2–3). From Babylonia he travelled to Phoenicia where he taught the Phoenicians 'the cycles of the sun and moon, and everything else as well' (9.17.4). When the Armenians ('the king of Shinar' according to Genesis 14.1) attacked the Phoenicians and captured Abraham's nephew, Abraham retaliated and took captive the children and women of the enemy. On being offered money for their release, he sent them back without ransom, for 'he chose not to make a profit out of the misery of others' (9.17.5). Thereafter, as guest of the City-Temple or Argarizin he received gifts from Melchizedek, 'its ruler and priest of God' (9.17.6). As a result of famine in the land, Abraham and his household moved on to Egypt where he 'lived in Heliopolis with the Egyptian priests and taught them much'. In particular, 'he explained astrology and the other sciences to them, saying that the Babylonians and he himself had obtained this knowledge', though its actual discovery was to be attributed to Enoch (9.17.8). Both here and in the anonymous fragment (see p. 69) Abraham's ancestry is traced to the giants who lived in the land of Babylonia. In this latter fragment it is re-iterated that 'after Abraham had learned astrology, he first went to Phoenicia and taught it to the Phoenicians (and) later he went to Egypt' (9.18.2). The lesson taught by both fragments is clear enough: Abraham's ancestry, his widespread journeyings and his knowledge of astrology, together with all other sciences, demonstrate that he, the father of the Hebrew people, was the teacher of both the Phoenicians and the Egyptians and consequently of the Greeks (cf. *Ant.* I.168) whose wisdom had been derived from these very two sources. In other words, the origins of the vaunted culture of the West were to be found not in these civilizations but rather in the biblical tradition and especially in Abraham whose wisdom enlightened all cultures other than his own.

An additional piece of information concerning Abraham comes from an early commentary on the Book of Genesis, the Genesis Apocryphon from Qumran. This presents our hero as an exorcist who drives out 'the scourge and the spirit of festering' from Pharaoh who had taken Sarah to be his wife: 'So I prayed [for him] . . . and I laid my hands on his [head], and the scourge departed from him and the evil [spirit] was expelled [from him], and he lived' (Col.XX).

In Jubilees 12.25–27 an account is given of Abraham reviving the use of Hebrew as a spoken and written language which, we are told, had ceased from the time of the overthrow of Babel. His mouth and ears were opened and he began to converse in Hebrew which is described as 'the tongue of creation'. 'And he took his father's books – and they were written in Hebrew – and he copied them. And he began studying them thereafter.' According to 10.14 Noah passed on his secret books to Shem who, according to Jewish tradition, passed them on to Abraham who studied in the school of Shem. No reference is made in our present chapter to this tradition, however; Abraham during 'six months of rain', studies the books of his forefathers (12.27, cf. also 21.10).

(b) A religious genius

Here again the Book of Jubilees provides us with much information, supplemented by a number of other pseudepigraphical writings.

In keeping with the biblical record itself, Jubilees records Abraham's perfect obedience to the word of God: 'For Abraham was perfect in all of his actions with the Lord and was pleasing through righteousness all the days of his life' (23.10). This righteousness was based on the fact that he had kept the whole Torah even when it was as yet unwritten (16.28, cf. Ecclus. 44.20; II Bar. 57.2). Indeed, it can be said that, such was the righteousness of Abraham, Isaac and Jacob and their obedience to the Law that, as we have already noted, they were without sin and in no need of repentance (Prayer of Manasseh 8).

Such obedience finds expression in many ways, but not least in his determined opposition to idolatry. He challenges his own father Terah and urges him to worship instead the God of heaven. But he and his brothers are afraid of the consequences and bid him keep silent (12.1–8). Then at last in the sixtieth year of his life he burns down 'the house of idols' (12.12ff.). He had been only fourteen years of age when he separated from his father and refused to worship the idols with him (11.16). From then on he was to teach the one, true and living God (20.7–10) who is holy, faithful and righteous (21.3–5, 21–25) and who alone is creator of heaven and earth (22.6). In later years Josephus the historian was to confirm Abraham's reputation in this regard: '(Abraham) was the first boldly to declare that God, the creator of the universe, is one, and that, if any other being contributed aught to man's welfare, each did so by His command and not in virtue of its own inherent power' (*Ant.* I.155). The same theme is taken up, as we shall see, in the Apocalypse of Abraham 1–8 where Abraham again takes a firm stand against idolatrous worship and practice.

His obedience is matched only by his trust in God and his faithfulness to his word (17.15). In the biblical story of the sacrifice of Isaac it is said that 'God tested Abraham' (Gen. 22.1). The writer of Jubilees uses this as a peg, as it were, on which to hang his own graphic account of how Abraham is subjected to ten tests or temptations (17.17f.) at the instigation of Mastema (17.16), the last of which had to do with the purchase of the cave at Machpelah in which to bury his dead (19.8). We see reflected here a Jewish tradition associated with the name of Abraham who had to endure ten trials but remained faithful to the end. As Pirke 'Aboth says, 'With ten temptations was Abraham

74

our father tempted, and he stood steadfast in them all, to show how great was the love of Abraham our father' (5.3). Or as Jubilees puts it, 'He was not impatient . . . and he was not filled with anxiety . . . He was found faithful, controlled of spirit' (19.3,8).

His faithfulness and righteousness are further illustrated by reference to the longevity of his life. In Genesis 25.7 it is said that the days of his life were one hundred and seventy-five years. This gives opportunity for the writer of Jubilees to point out that, although in antediluvian times the lives of the ancients were nineteen jubilees, in the time after the Flood people grew old much more quickly and the days of their lives were drastically shortened as a result of 'the evil of their ways' (23.8f.). But this was not so with Abraham, for 'he was perfect in all his actions' (23.10). It is true that his life was shorter than the antediluvian patriarchs, but the lives of those after him would be much shorter still because of sin (23.11ff.). But after much sin and tribulation people will 'begin to search the law . . . and return to the way of righteousness'. When that happens their 'days will begin to increase and grow longer' and 'approach a thousand years . . . All their days they will be complete and live in peace and rejoicing' (23.26ff.).

By reason of his enduring faithfulness God has made him the heir of his promises and has entered into a covenant with him and his successors for ever (1.7;12.22–24;13.3,19–21;14;15). As Ben Sira had said: 'Abraham was the great father of a multitude of nations . . . and was taken into covenant with him' (44.20).

According to IV Ezra 3.14f., not only did God make with him an everlasting covenant, he loved him and 'revealed (to him) the end of the times, secretly by night', thus opening the way for him and for Israel to eternal life.

(c) Heir of the covenant

In the Apocalypse of Abraham, the patriarch is again presented as a powerful opponent of idolatry and hence as the forefather of those who, with him, are heirs of the promise made by God in solemn covenant. His descendants are to be distinguished clearly from the Gentiles. They will suffer at their hands, but remain God's covenant people and will be vindicated at the end.

The book divides into two parts. Chapters 1–8 describe Abraham's opposition to idolatry, and chapters 9–32 contain the apocalypse proper. The first of these elaborates the account given in the Book of

75

Jubilees and makes a mockery of idol-worship. Abraham's father, Terah, is presented as an idol-maker who fashions gods from stone, metal and wood and sends out his son as a travelling salesman. An accident in which a stone idol loses its head and others are smashed to pieces, and a mis-adventure in which a wooden idol is burned in the fire convince Abraham that they are not gods at all, but objects of scorn. He then turns to 'the God who created all the gods supposed by us' and is bidden to leave his father's house. No sooner had he done so than the house was burned to the ground.

In the apocalypse that follows, Abraham is presented as a visionary to whom God says: 'I will announce to you guarded things and you will see great things which you have not seen' (9.6). Having offered up a sacrifice, as God commanded, he is met by the angel Yaoel, sent forth by God, who takes him up to heaven, carried on the wings of a pigeon and a turtledove which had been brought for the sacrifice (15.1ff.). There in a series of visions, he is shown the dwelling place of fiery angels (15.4ff), the chariot-throne of God 'with fiery wheels' (18.1ff., like that in Ezekiel 1), the seven-fold firmament with its 'multitude of heavenly angels' (19.4ff.), the earth beneath the firmament and on it 'a great crowd of men and women and children, half of them on the right side . . . and half of them on the left side' (21.1ff.), the Fall of Adam and its consequences for the human race (24.3ff.), the coming judgment and the destruction of the Temple brought about by the sin of idolatry and the people's perversion of the cult (27.1ff.). The time of deliverance (for the writer of the book) is near at hand, for 'the age' is to last for 'twelve hours', apparently of one hundred years each which, according to contemporary calculations (eg. by Josephus), began with the founding of Jerusalem by David and would end some time after its destruction in AD 70. The Gentiles ('those on the left side', cf. 21.7) will be judged by Abraham's descendants ('those on the right side') who will offer their sacrifices in the Temple in the new 'age of justice' soon to begin. Before that age dawns these Gentiles will be afflicted by ten plagues. But then, at the sound of the trumpet, God will send his 'chosen one' who will gather together the scattered people of Israel and burn with fire 'those who ruled over them in this age' (31.1ff.).

Abraham, then, is presented in this Apocalypse pre-eminently as one with whom God entered into covenant so that, in all generations to come, his descendants would be recognizably separate from the Gentiles. This separation is illustrated, and effected, by their rejection of idolatry and in particular by their avoidance of all shameful or evil cultic practices which would denigrate the name of God. Abraham had set a supreme example and could well be described as 'Abraham, friend of God who has loved you' (10.5) whose seed would be 'as the number of the stars' (20.5).

(d) Saintly, but severe

The Testament of Abraham is very different from the Apocalypse of that name in both content and tone. It survives in two recensions and in all probability is a Jewish work with Christian interpolations.

The scene is set during the last day of Abraham's life. He is presented as a good man who 'lived in quietness, gentleness and righteousness, and the righteous man was very hospitable'. This was shown clearly in the way this 'pious and entirely holy' man welcomed everyone, friends and strangers alike (1.1–2). Small wonder he was called 'God's beloved friend' (1.6) and a 'righteous soul elect of God' (2.3). With his righteousness, moreover, went riches for, by the blessing of God, he had 'a large livelihood and many possessions' (1.5) with a retinue of servants (2.1).

But there was one thing this righteous and powerful man could not evade – the approach of death! And so God sends Michael to tell him of his impending demise. At first Abraham does not recognize him as a heavenly visitor (though Isaac does) despite some mysterious happenings associated with him – a myrtle tree speaks with a human voice and Michael's tears turn into precious stones (3.3,11)! On being told of his approaching end, however, he is reluctant to give up his soul. This grudging attitude on the part of Abraham contrasts unfavourably with that ready obedience and confident faith we find in the biblical story and in, say, the Book of Jubilees. He asks that, before he dies, he might be allowed to see 'all the inhabited world and all the created things' (9.6). His request is granted and Michael lifts him up 'on a chariot of cherubim' so that he 'soared over the entire inhabited world' (10.1) and 'saw everything that was happening in the world' (10.3). So incensed is he by the obvious sinfulness of men on earth that he calls down fire from heaven and destroys many of them. God immediately orders Michael to stop the chariot and turn Abraham away lest he should see the sinfulness of all mankind and destroy everything that exists (10.12f.)! Because Abraham 'has not sinned . . . he has no mercy on sinners' (10.13). His very righteousness makes him completely insensitive towards all such. God, on the other hand,

77

is merciful and 'delays the death of the sinner until he should convert and live' (10.14).

God now orders that this severe and stubborn critic of sinners be taken up on a tour of heaven to see the process of divine judgment and, hopefully, to learn mercy from the experience. There he is shown a broad way and a narrow way leading into heaven along which the souls of men must pass. Many souls go through a broad gate and few through a narrow gate watched by Adam, the first man (11.1ff.). Some are tried by fire, others by recorded evidence and others again by weighing in the balance. Similarly, there are three judgments: one by Abel the son of Adam, the second by the tribes of Israel and the third by God himself (12.1–13.8). On seeing a soul whose sins and righteous deeds are equally balanced, Abraham suggests that they pray on its behalf. When they arise from prayer they find that an angel has taken the soul into Paradise (14.1–8). Encouraged by this, Abraham now intercedes for those sinners whom he had previously condemned. God hears his prayer and brings them back to life.

It is of interest to note that in this book judgment is meted out to Jew and Gentile alike and in each case the criterion is the 'sinful deeds' committed during their life-time. There is no escaping such judgment except by repentance and by premature death, for those who die before their time will not receive further punishment (14.15).

Michael now brings Abraham back to earth, bids him prepare his testament and return with him to God's presence. Again Abraham refuses to follow. God then sends his angel Death in disguise to take Abraham's soul. Though of 'abominable countenance and merciless look' he 'donned a most radiant robe . . . assuming the form of an archangel' (16.1ff.; cf. Test. of Isaac 2.4 where it is said that the archangel who appeared to Isaac 'resembled his father Abraham'). Death discloses his identity and reveals his mission, but Abraham refuses to go with him. Being challenged by Abraham, Death shows his 'terrible ferocity' which is so devastating that six thousand onlookers die on the spot (17.1ff.). Death repeats that he has come for Abraham's soul and invites him to kiss his hand. As soon as he had done so 'his soul cleaved to the hand of Death . . . for Death deceived him' (20.8f.). Michael then comes and carries his soul to heaven and his body is buried at the Oak of Mamre (20.10ff.).

The various pictures presented of Abraham in these writings are not altogether consistent with one another, reflecting as they do the different circumstances and expectations of the authors. But in them all he stands high as a great hero whose reputation and importance grow apace with the passing of the years.

3. Isaac

Frequent reference is made to Isaac throughout the pseudepigraphical writings, with particular reference to Abraham's intended sacrifice of him, the importance of the covenant and the fulfilment of God's promises to the children of Jacob. Of peculiar interest, however, is the Testament of Isaac, dating from the second century AD, which, in its existing form, shows marked Christian elements and commemorates the death of Isaac on a specific day in the Coptic Christian calendar. Despite this Christian setting, it is in all probability dependent on Jewish tradition and has a close affinity with the Testament of Abraham. The story it tells has wandered far from the biblical narrative and shows Isaac in a favourable light.

(a) A virtuous man

He is highly honoured by God, so much so that 'everyone who shall name his son after my beloved Isaac' will receive the divine blessing for ever (6.6,10), and anyone who spends a whole night 'commemorating my beloved Isaac without sleeping' will receive the heritage of the kingdom (6.14). Indeed, everything that is asked in the name of Isaac will be given 'as a covenant for ever' (6.8).

He is described as being 'like the silver which is burned, smelted, purified and refined in the fire' as are his descendants after him (8.3). When his father was ready to offer him as a sacrifice to God, it was as if 'the perfume of his sacrifice' ascended to the throne of God. And when the time came for him to depart from this life, it is observed that 'his soul . . . was white as snow' (7.1). A place has been prepared for him and for Abraham and Jacob in the kingdom of heaven. There they will be seated on thrones, for they 'shall be above everyone else in the kingdom' (2.7f.).

(b) A companion of angels

Following an opening dedication, the book begins with Isaac addressing his sons and the gathered company concerning the worthlessness of life on earth as contrasted with the glory of God's heavenly kingdom where even 'thieves and tax-collectors' may be received by a compassionate and merciful God 'because of the sincerity of their faith' (1.8).

Just then God sends his archangel Michael, for the time has come for Isaac's soul to depart from his body. Isaac is not taken by surprise, for 'it was customary every day for the holy angels to speak to him'; but he *is* surprised to observe that this archangel 'resembled his father Abraham' (2.1–4; cf. Test. of Jacob 2.4 where the archangel who appears there resembles Isaac). Assuring him that he is indeed Michael, the archangel gives him the reason for his visit and says that Abraham is waiting for him in heaven (2.5–16).

On hearing this, Isaac expresses concern for his son Jacob lest he be upset, but is assured he will be blessed and be the father of many nations and not only of the twelve tribes that will come forth from him (2.17ff.) for, together with Abraham and Jacob, he is to be 'father to all the world' (2.9). Michael departs and Isaac breaks the news to Jacob who is greatly distressed. Isaac comforts him, reminding him of his great ancestry and of his great future as progenitor of the twelve tribes [and of Jesus the Messiah] (3.1–19).

(c) An ascetic priest

Isaac is now presented as 'a priest of the Lord' (4.10) who lives a very ascetic life. He rises up in the middle of the night for prayer and continues in the day time also. So devoted to prayer is he that he declines to sleep in a bed. He fasts every day till evening and observes the three forty-day periods of fasting every year. He abstains from meat and wine and takes no fruit (4.1–6).

His reputation draws the crowds who flock to hear his teaching. He tells them to be pure in heart and in body, guarding themselves against slander and evil of every kind (4.11–17). He has a special word for the priests among them, for 'the work of the priesthood is not easy' (4.41). When making an offering they are to be ritually and morally pure, not allowing their thoughts to be diverted by worldly affairs. They must persevere in piety, 'expending all their efforts and their lives in prayer'. They will be engaged in 'holy, angelic service', knowing that 'their earthly conduct will be reflected in heaven, and the angels will be their friends' (4.19–54).

(d) A visitor to the other world

His address being ended, Isaac is now taken by an angel to visit first hell, then heaven (5.4ff.). In hell he sees the terrible tortures and anguish of the wicked who are at the mercy of wild beasts (5.10–20), who burn in a river of fire (5.21–25) and are plunged into a deep abyss (5.26f.). He is then taken to heaven where he sees Abraham 'and all the godly ones'. Conversation ensues in which God indicates that his blessing is on those who repent and pray, who feed the poor and who commemorate his 'beloved Isaac' (6.1–23).

God's discourse being ended, he calls on Michael who mounts 'the chariot of the seraphim' and, with a retinue of angels before him, sets off to claim the soul of Isaac. On seeing Michael and all the saints and angels who accompany him, Isaac is full of joy; but Jacob weeps and Isaac comforts him (6.24–35). Isaac's soul is then carried up to heaven in the holy chariot and God bestows on him the blessings of the kingdom (7.1–2). And so the book ends with an exhortation to keep 'the memorial day' of Isaac for ever and assuring the devout of a place in the kingdom for ever (8.1–9.1).

4. Jacob

The Testament of Jacob has a great deal in common with the Testament of Isaac and presents the same scenario of an angel coming for the partriarch's soul, his tour of hell and heaven, his moral teaching to his children (put into the mouth of the narrator) and the need for help on the day of judgment. This is supplemented by the Ladder of Jacob which describes the biblical vision of angels ascending and descending, adding the detail that on the ladder are twelve steps and on the left and right of each a human face, twenty-four in all. The twelve steps are the twelve periods into which the age is divided, and the twenty-four faces are of Gentile kings who will put Jacob's descendants to the test. Further supplement is given in the Prayer of Jacob (first to fourth century AD) and in the Prayer of Joseph (first century AD) which have something in common with certain Jewish magical texts and refer to the secret name of God.

Without repeating the characteristic marks of Isaac already indicated which apply in the main to Jacob, we may note a few distinguishing features about him in these books:

(a) A man of moral rectitude

Jacob is not presented as an ascetic in the way that Isaac is, but he is equally strong in his defence of high moral standards. Some of his teaching coincides with that of Isaac; at other times the emphases are new or different. His offspring are to study the Torah and emulate the patriarchs. They must avoid anger and depravity, injustice and blasphemy, sexual immorality and homosexuality, gluttony and idolatry. Those who commit such sins will not come near the kingdom (Test. of Jacob 7.2ff.).

(b) A man of prayer

Jacob is presented as a man of prayer in all three of the documents that bear his name. In the Testament it is said of him that he used to resort to 'a secluded place' where he would 'offer his prayers before the Lord in the night and in the day' (1.9). He encourages the practice of prayer on the part of his hearers (7.17) and indicates how much they owe to the prayers of the patriarchs on their behalf (7.11) as well as to the prayers of the saints (7.21;8.3,8), not least on the day of judgment (8.5). The Prayer of Jacob may refer to the secret name of God (15), but it is addressed to the 'Father of the Patriarchs' (1) who is the creator of all things (2), and in the Ladder of Jacob he is the thrice-holy God (3.18) who carries the whole world under his arm (2.9) and is in control of all the constellations of heaven (2.12ff.).

The memory of Jacob, like that of Isaac, is to be honoured; and blessed are all those who keep their memorial day, for they are saints well-pleasing to God (8.1f.).

(c) A companion of angels

Here again the Testament of Jacob has a lot in common with that of Isaac. It is said, for example, that it was Jacob's custom, like Isaac before him, every day to speak with the angels (1.7). It was no surprise to him to be informed that the angel who now spoke with him was his guardian angel who had watched over him at home (1.10) and had accompanied him on his journey to Egypt and saved him from the hand of Esau (2.10f.). What *did* surprise – and frighten – him was the fact that this angel resembled his father Isaac: 'he lifted up his eyes toward the radiance of the angel who was speaking to him, who was in appearance and in face like his father Isaac' (III. 1 Coptic text).

It is of interest to note that just as in the Testament of Isaac an angel appears to Isaac in the form of (his father) Abraham (2.3) and in the Testament of Jacob to Jacob in the form of (his father) Isaac (2.4), so, it would seem, in the Prayer of Joseph he appears to Joseph in the form of (his father) Jacob (Fragment A 1,4). In the first two cases the angel is presumably Michael; in the third case he is named as 'Israel, an angel of God' (A1). Joseph is addressed in these words: 'I, Jacob, who is speaking to you, am also Israel, an angel of God and a ruling spirit . . . I, Jacob, whom men call Jacob but whose name is Israel am he whom God called Israel which means, a man seeing God, because I am the firstborn of every living thing to whom God gives life . . . Uriel, the angel of God, came forth and said that I [Jacob-Israel] had descended to earth and I had tabernacled among men and that I had been called by the name Jacob . . . Am I not Israel, the first minister before the face of God' (Prayer of Joseph A 1–9). We observe that in certain magical and mystical texts Israel is presented as an angel; here in the Prayer of Joseph it is the heavenly name of which its earthly counterpart is 'Jacob'. Commenting on this passage, J. Z. Smith describes the Prayer of Joseph as 'a myth of the mystery of Israel' and adds: 'Whether the earthly Jacob-Israel is to be understood as a thoroughly docetic figure, the incarnation of a heavenly power, or a heavenly messenger is not clear'. He sees the Prayer situated within a 'circle of first-century Judaism which sought a model for salvation in the ascent of the patriarchs to the full reality of their heavenly, angelic nature' and points to 'the complete pattern' in II Enoch where Enoch the man (1.1ff.) ascended to heaven to become an angel (22.9f.), came back to earth (36.1) and finally returned to his angelic state in heaven (36.1;67.2) (in J. H. Charlesworth (ed), *The Old Testament Pseudepigrapha* vol. 2, pp. 704f.).

Elsewhere, as in the Ladder of Jacob, angels play a prominent part. But the Prayer of Jacob is of greater significance still. The most relevant section reads as follows:

> Fill me with wisdom,
> empower me, Lord.
> Fill my heart with good things, Lord;
> as an earthly angel,
> as having become immortal,
> as having received the gift which is from you (17–19).

J. H. Charlesworth suggests that the fourth line, in keeping with those that follow, may be best translated, 'as (having become) an earthly angel'. This would agree with certain references in the Qumran texts and in a number of the pseudepigrapha which 'demonstrate that Jews could have thought of a righteous person on earth becoming an angel and asking for wisdom and power' (ibid., p. 723, note i 2). If this is so, we are to understand such ideas as belonging to that same 'circle of first century Judaism' to which reference was made above.

VII

The Twelve Patriarchs

1. The twelve

We have already considered a number of 'testamentary-style' books, written during or after the intertestamental period, which both commemorate and extol the patriarchs of old who were said to exemplify the most highly-prized virtues and so to provide an example and inspiration to God's people living at the time of the books' appearing. The most comprehensive of these is the Testaments of the XII Patriarchs which, in its present form, shows clear Christian influence, but probably in its original form is to be traced back, in part at least, to the second century BC. In terms of content and form, it has an affinity with the Book of Jubilees and a number of fragments from Qumran, particularly fragments of an Aramaic Testament of Levi.

Following the pattern of Jacob's final 'testament' as recorded in Genesis 49, in which the patriarch on his deathbed addresses his sons, the Testaments of the XII Patriarchs, in like manner, introduces Jacob's twelve sons in turn. The general pattern followed is in three parts: a description of significant events in the life of the patriarch concerned with particular reference to his own moral rectitude or otherwise, an exhortation in the light of the disclosures just made encouraging his sons not to fall into the same errors or to emulate his example as the case may be, and a prediction concerning what will happen to his sons or the tribes they represent right up to the last days.

Throughout the book emphasis is laid on two matters in particular which are closely related to each other: ethical exhortation and eschatological expectation. The first of these is evident in all the 'Testaments' of the sons of Jacob and finds its chief exemplar in

85

Joseph; the second finds expression in a very special way in the persons of Levi and Judah from whom will come salvation in the last days.

(a) The sons of Jacob: an ethical ideal

On a number of occasions stress is laid on demands for social righteousness, as in the Testament of Benjamin 10.3 where the patriarch's sons are exhorted to show truth and righteousness towards their neighbours, for their attitude to their neighbours reflects their attitude to God. But more often than not the appeal is to those virtues which the Stoics, for example, would have recognized as marks of 'the ideal man', qualities of character like self-control, integrity, compassion, generosity and the cultivation of a balanced life. This is well presented in the words of Jacob's twelfth son, Benjamin: 'See then, my children, what is the goal of the good man. Be imitators of him in his goodness because of his compassion, in order that you may wear crowns of glory. For a good man does not have a blind eye, but he is merciful to all, even though they may be sinners. And even if persons plot against him for evil ends, by doing good this man conquers evil, being watched over by God. He loves those who wrong him as he loves his own life. If anyone glorifies himself, he holds no envy. If anyone becomes rich, he is not jealous. If anyone is brave, he praises him. He loves the moderate person; he shows mercy to the impoverished; to the ill he shows compassion; he fears God. He loves the person who has the gift of a good spirit as he loves his own life' (4.1–5).

Sin in the human heart is caused by Beliar who represents 'the spirit of error' in its fight against 'the spirit of truth'. But this does not excuse men for the error of their ways: it is in their power to subdue anger, greed and envy and to avoid drunkenness and promiscuity. All such things deny that brotherly-love which is the chief test of the ideal man. Such virtue is true wisdom (Test. of Levi 13.7f.); in particular it will oppose idolatry which is a denial of God, and homosexuality which is a departure from 'the order of nature' (Test. of Napht. 3.4) which God himself ordained.

This quality of brotherly love, like so many of the other virtues mentioned, has its supreme exemplar in Joseph who guarded himself against jealousy and envy and lived in the integrity of his heart (Test. of Sim. 4.5). He is one who found favour before God and man (Test. of Reub. 4.8), a good man full of compassion and mercy who loved his brothers as his own life (Test. of Sim. 4.4,6); nothing evil resided in him (Test. of Zeb. 8.4); he was a good and pious man (Test. of Dan 1.4; Test. of Benj. 3.1), made all the more illustrious by reason of his trials (Test. of Benj. 5.5). Benjamin's portrait of the 'ideal man' given above was not just an imaginary picture drawn at random. The man in the studio of his imagination was none other than Joseph, the sum total, the very embodiment, of all virtue (Test. of Benj. 4.1–5).

This portrait finds particular expression in the Testament that bears his name. The account given there is based on the biblical story of Joseph and the seductions of Potiphar's wife (the name appears as Pentephres in this book) and, in an elaborated form, illustrates his virtuous qualities of faithful endurance and unswerving love towards his brothers. In a poetic introduction he refers to 'ten testings' he had to endure which called forth the 'powerful medicine' of endurance (2.6). This is illustrated in the story that follows (3.1–9.5) which tells how he had to struggle against the wiles of 'a shameless woman' who at first pretended to mother him, then sought religious instruction from him, then offered to get rid of her husband, then 'doctored' his food, then threatened suicide and finally brought false accusations against him so that he was thrown into prison. But through it all Joseph remained faithful in prayer and strong in self-control. With such a record he is able to counsel his own children to 'pursue self-control and purity with patience, and prayer with fasting in humility of heart' (10.2).

A second narrative (10.5–16.6) illustrates the supreme quality of love towards others, not least to those who have wronged him. Having been sold to the Ishmaelites as a slave, he refused to disclose his identity as son of Jacob, 'a great person in the sight of God and men', lest by so doing he might disgrace his brothers, and when eventually the eunuch in Pentephris's employ over-charged his master for his purchase price, for the same reason he refused to report him, but kept silent.

Accordingly he is able to admonish his own children to 'love one another and in patient endurance conceal one another's shortcomings' (17.2). Just as God had exalted him, so he would exalt them and they would be rescued from every evil (18.2). His own marriage to 'the daughter of the priest of Heliopolis' and all the rewards this brought in its train, is an illustration of how God rewards righteousness (18.3ff.). Chapter 19 describes a dream of the division of the twelve tribes, which is in all probability a Christian interpolation, and ends with an account of Joseph's death (20.1–6).

The patriarchs then, exemplified by Joseph the righteous man, acknowledge their own shortcomings and the need to live a virtuous life. One by one they commend such a life to their children with the assurance that God will enable them and will give them their proper reward in due time.

(b) Levi and Judah: God's anointed

The future hope of the sons of Jacob is bound up in a peculiar way with the persons of Levi and Judah together with their descendants. In this connection, it is clear, not only from its frequent usage but also from internal evidence, that the Testament of Levi (together with the Testament of Judah) shows evidence of the importance placed on these two patriarchs during the intertestamental period. Thus, fragments of an Aramaic version of a Testament of Levi were discovered in the Cairo Genizah and published in 1910 and several other such fragments have since come to light at Qumran. The Testament of Levi differs from the others that accompany it in that it is more taken up with eschatological than with ethical concerns. A cursory glance at the two Testaments of Levi and Judah indicates the central place they held in the expectations of that time.

First, the Testament of Levi. Having summoned his children he tells them how, in his sleep, he had seen a vision in which he was escorted by an angel to the heavenly world. There he is told he is to be God's priest who will 'tell forth his mysteries to man' (1.1–2.12). In the uppermost heaven is 'the Great Glory' before whose majesty all tremble; but Levi and his family will be blest (3.1–4.6). He sees 'the Holy Most High' sitting on his throne and is assured of 'the blessing of the priesthood' (5.1–7). He then returns to earth where, in company with Simeon, the angel orders him to destroy Shechem for the rape of his sister Dinah (7.1–4).

In a second vision he is given 'the vestments of the priesthood, the crown of righteousness, the oracle of understanding, the robe of truth, the breastplate of faith, the mitre for the head and the apron for prophetic power' (8.2). He is then anointed with holy oil and crowned with the priestly diadem, the climax of his investiture as 'priest for the Lord God' (8.4ff.).

His father Jacob now counsels him to avoid promiscuity (9.9) and to keep himself also ritually pure (9.11ff.), for by neglect of such things his descendants will 'defile the sanctuary'. Levi in turn admonishes his own sons to honour the Law of God and to be true to their priestly calling (13.1–9). An account is then given of the sins of the priesthood (reflecting no doubt the situation as seen by the writer in his own day) which will merit only 'scorn and eternal humiliation' (14.1–17.11). There will come a time when 'the priesthood will lapse'; but 'then the Lord will raise up a new priest' (18.1f.) who will have qualities usually ascribed to the promised *Davidic* deliverer:

There will be peace in all the earth . . .
In his priesthood sin shall cease
and lawless men shall rest from their evil deeds,
and righteous men shall find rest in him,
and he shall open up the gates of paradise (18.4,9f.).

From such passages, then, we see the messianic hope finding expression in Levi the priest and in his priestly descendants, a hope that in some way is shared also by the covenanters of Qumran (see below).

Secondly, there is the Testament of Judah. Here the patriarch tells his sons of his perfect obedience to his father resulting in his being designated king (1.5f; cf. 17.5f.), of his great exploits as hunter (2.1–7) and warrior (3.1–7, 10; 9.1–8) and gives the credit to an angel who accompanies him everywhere (3.10). His marriage to Bathshua, daughter of the king of Adullam, had illustrated his tendency to promiscuity under the influence of drink (8.1–3), and fornication is condemned not least in an account of his own and his sons' relations with his daughter-in-law Tamar (10.1–12.12). Allusion is made again to Judah's kingship both here and in later passages where Judah offers to pay Tamar with 'my staff, my ring, my royal crown as a pledge' (12.4; cf. 15.3f.) and where he confesses that 'women have the mastery over both king and poor man' (15.5f.).

In the light of his own experience he urges his sons to resist sensual passions, to beware of the enticements of money, to avoid the excesses of drunkenness and to shun promiscuity with which drunkenness is so closely associated (13.1–16.4), for by such things as these the kingdom of Judah will be diminished (17.3). It is his deepest regret that, in a state of drunkenness, he had disclosed to a Canaanite woman 'the commandments of God and the mysteries of Jacob, my father, which God has told me not to reveal' (16.4). It is not said what these 'mysteries' were, but the reference suggests that the origin of the Testament may have been in some Jewish esoteric sect.

Further exhortation against promiscuity and the love of money

(18.1–19.4) leads on to a short dissertation on 'the two spirits' which struggle for the mastery of the human heart: the spirit of truth and the spirit of error (19.1–4). The spirit of truth not only exhorts the righteous to good conduct, it also accuses the unrighteous before God (20.1–5).

There then follows an exhortation to 'love Levi', for to Judah God has given the kingship, but to Levi the priesthood to which the kingship is subjected (21.1–2); for just as heaven is superior to earth, 'so is God's priesthood superior to the kingdom on earth' (21.4). The kings who are to rule over Israel are condemned together with the licentiousness and idolatry of the people which will lead to the destruction of God's Temple by fire and their enslavement by the Gentiles. By penitence and 'integrity of heart' they will at last be freed from captivity (21.6–23.5).

This time of deliverance will be marked by the coming of the Davidic messianic king who is described as 'a Star from Jacob', 'the Sun of righteousness', 'the Shoot of God Most High', 'the fountain for the life of all humanity'. He will walk in gentleness and righteousness; no sin will be found in him; the Spirit will be poured out on him and he will pour out the spirit of grace on the sons of Jacob (24.1–6); Abraham, Isaac and Jacob, together with the righteous, will be resurrected; authority will be given to the sons of Jacob, pre-eminently to Levi and then to Judah, and 'all the people shall glorify the Lord for ever' (25.1–5). Having bidden his children 'observe the whole Law', Judah dies and is buried in Hebron with his fathers (26.1–4).

These two Testaments reflect certain strongly felt beliefs among some at least of the Jews at the time of writing and may have in mind hopes (and fears) associated with the priestly/kingly House of the Hasmoneans. One of these beliefs is that the priesthood, deriving from Levi, is of divine origin (cf. also Jub. 31.13ff.) and must keep itself pure both morally and ritually and so honour the Law of God. The sins of the priesthood will bring judgment on the people's heads; but God will bring rest and peace through 'a new priest' whom he will raise up to be their deliverer. He will effect salvation 'and there shall be peace in all the earth'; 'the glory of the Most High shall burst forth upon him and the spirit of understanding and sanctification shall rest upon him'; the very angels will rejoice because of him; he will remove the sword; because of him the nations will be illumined; Beliar will be bound and wicked spirits trampled underfoot; and 'all the saints will be clothed in righteousness' (Test. of Levi 18.1–14).

A second belief is that Judah will be the forebear of a royal house which will produce the promised messianic king (Test. of Judah 17.5f.; 22.2f.; 24.1–6), a belief echoed elsewhere and most specifically in the Psalms of Solomon (17.23–51; 18.6–10). Subsequent Jewish literature and the evidence of the Gospels show how popular was this expectation of a messianic deliverer from the House of David.

But the Testaments give evidence of a third belief, that God would in fact raise up *two* deliverers, one to act as priest and one to act as king in the coming kingdom. There is no unanimity among scholars concerning such 'double messianism', but this concept is in harmony with the teaching of the book as a whole which joins together the *tribes* of Levi and Judah as the agents of God's deliverance and asserts that 'the Lord will raise up from Levi someone as high priest and from Judah someone as king . . . (who) will save all the gentiles and the tribe of Israel' (Test. of Simeon 7.1f.). Such belief in a priestly deliverer and a kingly deliverer would be seen to have precedent in the joint leadership of Joshua and Zerubbabel at the time of the building of the second Temple (cf. Zech. 3–4) and finds expression in a body like the Covenanters at Qumran. In the Rule of the Community, for example, the members of that Community are to live according to the agreed discipline 'until there shall come a prophet and the Messiahs of Aaron and Israel' (IX. 11). This third eschatological figure, 'a prophet', features quite prominently in the scrolls and is alluded to also, alongside the priest and the king, in the Testaments (cf. Test. of Benj. 9.2; see pp. 123ff.). Again, in both scrolls and Testaments it is suggested that precedence is given to the priestly deliverer over the kingly deliverer as agent of God's redemption (for a fuller treatment of the notion of 'double messanism', see my *The Method and Message of Jewish Apocalyptic*, 1964, pp. 310–323).

2. Joseph

The book entitled 'Joseph and Aseneth' (first century BC – second century AD) has been described as a romantic novel. It is this – and more besides. It was written to explain how it came about that Joseph, a paragon of Hebrew virtue, had come to marry a foreign woman who worshipped idols (cf. Gen. 41.45) and tells how this woman Aseneth, daughter of an idolatrous priest of Heliopolis in Egypt, turned from idolatry to worship 'the living God'. It is in fact a religious tract with a strong appeal to Gentile converts like the heroine of the book.

The plot of the story can be told briefly. Aseneth, at eighteen years of age, is a beautiful virgin, much sought after by suitors including the Pharaoh's son. She rejects them all and shows the same disdain for Joseph who is recommended by her father Pentephres (4.5–12). She changes her mind, however, when she sees him dressed in an exquisite white tunic and purple robe with a golden crown on his head (5.1–6.8). As she goes forward to kiss him, Joseph restrains her saying that 'it is not fitting for a man who worships God . . . to kiss a strange woman who will bless with her mouth dead and dumb idols' (8.5). He then prays for her conversion and departs with the promise of an early return. Aseneth forthwith repents in sackcloth and ashes, throws away her idols and goes into mourning, fasting for seven days (9.1–10.17). On the eighth day God's chief angel appears to her, assuring her that her name is in 'the book of the living,' that she has been 'made alive again', that she will henceforth represent 'a city of refuge' (for all such converts as herself), and that she will marry Joseph. At the angel's bidding she eats a miraculous honeycomb representing the bread of life (16.16), drinks 'a cup of immortality' and is anointed with 'ointment of incorruptibility'. He then disappears and returns to heaven (14.1–17.10). The scene is set for Joseph's return. Aseneth dresses herself in her finest gown and goes to meet him. She tells him of her conversion and they embrace. Three times Joseph kisses her and she receives 'the spirit of life', 'the spirit of wisdom' and 'the spirit of truth' (19.11). Thus prepared, she is married to Joseph by Pharaoh himself (18.1–21.9).

The second part of the narrative begins with the re-appearance of Pharaoh's son who, after eight years, still has designs on Aseneth. Failing to persuade Simeon and Levi to murder Joseph, he enlists the support of Dan and Gad to do so and to kidnap Aseneth; but his evil designs are thwarted by Simeon, Levi and Benjamin. Aseneth intercedes for the wrong-doers with Levi and his brothers and pardons them. The story ends with the death of Pharaoh's son, who had been mortally wounded in the fray. Pharaoh himself dies and Joseph reigns in his stead (23.1–29.9).

(a) A model of virtue

It is clear that the chief character in the story is Aseneth who, in her converted state, shows qualities in her dealings with her would-be kidnappers that show her worthy to be Joseph's wife. Her brother-in-law Levi also shows up well, refusing to render evil for evil (23.9; 29.3) or to take advantage of another in distress (23.12; 29.3).

The figure of Joseph is less prominent than that of his bride but, as in the case of the Testaments though with less conviction, he is presented as a model of virtue, albeit rather formal and stilted in presentation. He belongs to 'the upper crust' of society and shows the gifts and graces of his class, with a certain aloofness that makes him appear 'whiter than white'. He is introduced as 'Joseph the Powerful One of God' and 'chief of the whole land of Egypt' who 'worships God, (is) self-controlled and a virgin . . . a man powerful in wisdom and experience and the spirit of God is upon him' (4.7; 18.1). He is 'meek and merciful and fearing God' (8.8), and so he deals mercifully with Aseneth, praying for her conversion from idolatry to worship of the true God (8.9ff.). So strict is he in his religious observance that he will not sit at table with non-Jews (7.1); far less will he dream of marrying a woman who is an idolatress (8.7). Morally too he is pure, always acting properly towards the opposite sex (8.1,5) and refusing to sleep with a woman who is not his wife (21.1). The picture presented in the Testament of Joseph is thus filled out and his character established as a veritable paragon of virtue.

(b) A son of God

In a number of places in this book Joseph is referred to by others as 'son of God' (6.3,5), 'your son' (13.13), 'his first-born son' (18.11; 21.4) and 'first-born son of God' (23.10). The expression, however, may not be quite so startling as it might at first sight appear. The fact is that in the Greek mythology of the time, it was used fairly commonly to describe legendary heroes and, in Egypt particularly, was a designation used of the Ptolemaic rulers. Within Jewish culture the Old Testament usage of the term to describe angels or heavenly beings was continued and developed within the Judaism of the post-biblical period. Philo, the Jewish philosopher contemporary with Jesus, could call the Logos God's 'image' or 'his first-born' or even 'the second God', and in the Wisdom of Solomon and elsewhere it denoted the righteous man (cf.2.16,18;5.5, etc) who is God's exemplar. So too in Ben Sira where those who befriend the fatherless and the widows are called 'sons' of God (4.10), and in the Dead Sea scrolls similar language is used of the Messiah who is the most righteous one of all. In these scrolls, moreover, members of the Qumran community are called 'sons of (God's) truth' and the angels are described as 'sons of heaven'.

In this book, Joseph and Aseneth, Joseph is presented as an outstanding example of 'the righteous man' and at the same time shows angel-like qualities. He is not himself a heavenly being but he possesses supernatural vision, for 'nothing hidden escapes him, because of the great light that is inside him' (6.6). The bride who is prepared for him has to be a very special person, endowed with supernatural beauty (18.9), who has eaten the miraculous honeycomb which is the bread of life (that heavenly manna which is the food of angels), has 'drunk a cup of immortality and been anointed with ointment of incorruptibility' (16.16). When the archangel descends from heaven to speak with Aseneth she sees him as 'a man in every respect similar to Joseph' (14.9). This may mean no more than that the archangel held second place to God as Joseph did to Pharaoh; but even if this is so, the very comparison with one whose 'face was like lightning' and whose 'eyes were like sunshine' (14.9) demonstrates those heavenly qualities his virtue displays.

VIII

Two Lawgivers: Moses and Ezra

1. The Moses sources

It is quite obvious that the figure of Moses was of considerable importance throughout the entire intertestamental period, both in Palestine and in Egypt, and is given frequent mention in a number of diverse sources. One of these is Artapanus, a Jewish writer who lived in Egypt, perhaps around the close of the third century BC, and who showed syncretistic tendencies in his understanding and practice of the Jewish religion. Three fragments of his work remain to us, relating respectively to Abraham, Joseph and (at somewhat greater length) Moses. Or, more accurately, they are three fragments from the historian Eusebius's *Praeparatio Evangelica* who quotes Alexander Polyhistor who, in turn, had summarized the work of Artapanus around the middle of the first century BC.

A second source is the dramatic presentation by Ezekiel the Tragedian entitled 'Exagōgē' which tells the story of Moses and the exodus from Egypt. It was written in Egypt, is probably to be dated in the first part of the second century BC and is dependent on an early recension of the Septuagint to which it adds, with dramatic effect, certain imaginative episodes and fictional characters. The text survives in fragments quoted by Eusebius (*Praeparatio Evangelica* 9. 28–29), Clement of Alexandria (*Strom.* 1.23.155f.) and Pseudo-Eustathius (*Commentarius in Hexaemeron*, PG 18,729).

A third source is represented by five fragments of the work of Aristobulus, an Alexandrian Jewish philosopher belonging to the middle of the first century BC, which are also preserved by Eusebius. These concern, in turn, the date of the Passover, the use of anthropomorphisms in the sacred writings, the dependence of Greek poets and philosophers on the Jewish Law, reasoning concerning the nature of God and finally the significance of the Sabbath within a cosmic setting.

A fourth source consists also of five fragments by a Jewish historian Eupolemus who probably lived in Palestine around the middle of the second century BC. The first of these fragments concerns Moses and so is relevant to our purpose here. As in the case of the works of Artapanus and Aristobulus, these fragments are not direct quotations but are recordings by Eusebius of summaries of these sources made by Alexander Polyhistor.

The most important source, however, for a study of the character of Moses during this period, is the Book of Jubilees written by a Jew living in Palestine about the middle of the second century BC. It is a form of *midrash* on Genesis and Exodus 1–12 and is written in the form of a revelation given to Moses on Mount Sinai during the forty days he spent there. It consists, in the main, of a description of past history and future events culminating in the appearance of the messianic kingdom. The book derives its name from its system of dividing history into 'jubilee' periods, each of forty-nine years, which in turn are sub-divided into seven weeks of years. In its commentary on the biblical text it makes free use of *haggadic* material in the form of story and legend, is not afraid to alter or change the emphasis of passages which might prove embarrassing or derogatory and is ready to amplify or supplement the sacred text in the interests of the author's purpose in writing, namely, to expound the eternal validity of the Law and not least its significance for the days in which the writer and his readers were then living. The author himself seems to have been of priestly stock who laid great store by the Law, not least its ritual observance. In this connection, it was of great importance that the festivals, for example, should fall on the same day each year, and so he advocated a solar year which would make this possible and opposed a calendar based on a lunar month which, on his argument, would lead only to confusion and breach of the law of God.

The Testament of Moses is yet another source which appears in certain ancient lists alongside an Assumption of Moses. The book as now preserved usually bears this second name, but is of the nature of a Testament. The final section is missing which, it has been suggested, may have belonged to a separate Assumption of Moses and have given an account of Moses' assumption to heaven. Its place of origin is no doubt Palestine, but there is division of opinion concerning its structure and date. R. H. Charles argued that there is a dislocation of the text and that chapters 8 and 9 (which reflect Antiochus's persecution) should be replaced between chapters 5 and 6 and on this basis postulated a date in the first century AD. This date is accepted by perhaps the majority of scholars. J. Licht and G. W. E. Nickelsburg, however, have argued for a Maccabean date for the bulk of the book and for a date in the time of Herod for a 'revised version' which, by means of inserted chapters 6 and 7, sought to give a re-interpretation in the light of the events of that time. The book consists of a farewell address by Moses just prior to his death based on Deuteronomy 31–34 and is in the form of a prediction of events from the entry into the promised land until the time of the end. The writer thus shows a deep interest in eschatology which demonstrates that God's kingdom 'will appear throughout all his creation' (10.1) and that Israel will be exalted 'to the heaven of the stars' (10.9).

The final source to be mentioned is that of Pseudo-Philo's Book of Biblical Antiquities, produced in Palestine during the first century AD. This is a comprehensive work which tells in its own way the story of Israel from Adam to David, making ample use of legendary tales to interpret and expound the biblical narrative. This is illustrated in the account given of Moses in chapters 9–19 which makes full use of the biblical story, but amplifies it by means of traditional and legendary material. Thus, in its treatment of the biblical text it has much in common with the Book of Jubilees and the Genesis Apocryphon from Qumran.

2. The Moses tradition

The picture of Moses which emerges from these writings reflects the varied hopes and expectations not only of the several authors but also of the Jewish communities living at that time in the different religious and cultural environments of Egypt and Palestine.

(a) The founder of culture

The legendary character of Moses is set forth most plainly in fragment three of Artapanus (*Praeparatio Evangelica* 9.27.1–37). There he is presented as the founder of culture in its many varied forms. It was he, for example, who contributed to Egyptian civilization the 'inventions' of navigation, structural engineering, irrigation, military equipment and even the Egyptian form of worship and who at the same time introduced the study of philosophy (27.4). Perhaps the most surprising of these is the reference to worship: having divided Egypt into 36 nomes, he then appointed for them and for their priests gods to be worshipped in the shape of 'cats, dogs and ibises' (27.5). No doubt we are to see here an over-zealous attempt to defend the Jews against the anti-Jewish writings of the Egyptian, Manetho (c. 280 BC), who asserted that Moses forbade the worship of such gods and at the same time an attempt to glorify Moses and so to give to the Jewish people a pride in their ethnic heritage. It is nevertheless strange, to say the least, to find a Jewish writer (albeit deeply influenced by the syncretism of his day) crediting Moses with the origination of animal worship. On the other hand, it should be noted that, although Artapanus regards such things as acceptable within the common culture, they will in fact be destroyed in the end together with the Egyptians in the waters of the Red Sea (27.35,37).

Moses' influence on Egyptian culture and civilization is matched only by that of Greece. This is demonstrated in the relationship he has with three mythical figures of high esteem. First, he is said to be identified with Mousaeus, the singer of Greek legend who was taught by Orpheus, the legendary founder of Orphism. Now the roles are reversed, for it is Moses who is the teacher and Orpheus who is the taught (27.3f.). Moses is thus the architect of Greek wisdom and culture. Secondly, he is to be identified with the god Hermes, son of Zeus, the herald of the gods whose staff became a magic wand: as such Moses is 'deemed worthy of godlike honour by the priests' (27.6;cf.Ex.7.1 where Moses is said to be 'a God to Pharaoh'). Since the Greek Hermes is to be identified with the Egyptian Thoth who invented writing and is the founder of the arts and sciences, this is further confirmation that Moses (= Hermes) is the architect of Egyptian as well as Greek wisdom and culture. Thirdly, he is related indirectly, through the Pharaoh's daughter, to the tradition of the great goddess Isis (27.3,15f.) who, according to well-established legend, had been taught by Hermes: thus Moses, as Hermes, is greater even than the great goddess herself! This superiority of Moses over Isis is illustrated still further in the use he makes of his rod in striking the earth and bringing forth plagues on Egypt, for the earth that is struck is none other than Isis herself on whom depends the creative power of the soil, and the rod is the very symbol dedicated to her honour by the priests in every temple (27.32). But, although Moses possessed all these 'godlike' qualities, this must not detract from the claim that God alone is 'the master of the universe' (27.22) whose divine voice speaks with authority (27.21) and at the mention of whose name men fall down speechless to the ground (27.24ff.).

(b) An idealized hero

Artapanus describes Moses, moreover, as 'altogether excellent' (27.7) and loved by the masses (27.6). In appearance he was 'tall, ruddy, gray with long hair, most venerable' who was able to carry out great exploits even at the advanced age of 89 years (27.37). One of these was an Egyptian expedition against the Ethiopians in which Moses, as commander-in-chief, led a peasant army of 100,000 men (27.8). He gained there a notable victory and founded on the site the city of Heliopolis. In the process, it is said, 'he made the ibis sacred because it destroys the creatures which harm men' (27.8;cf.*Ant.* II.245ff. where Josephus records how Moses took ibises with him in baskets and set them loose to destroy the serpents in the wilderness). Even these Ethiopians loved Moses and learned from him the rite of circumcision (27.10).

Other 'exploits' are mentioned which further enhance his reputation, sometimes by altering or modifying the biblical story in his favour. Thus, in his act of slaying the Egyptian it is reported that this was done in self-defence when his assailant drew a dagger to kill him (27.18). For good measure, the comment is added that the king of Memphis who had hatched the plot against Moses contracted elephantiasis and died (27.20). Fearing for his life, Moses fled to Arabia where he lived with Raguel (called Jethro in Ex.3.1) whose daughter he married. There, in due course, he saw a miraculous fire burning, although there was no wood or other kindling material on it (no mention is made of a bush) and heard a voice telling him to return to Egypt and rescue his people. On arriving in Egypt he was thrown into prison, but in the course of the night the doors miraculously opened of their own accord (27.23; cf. Acts 5.17ff.). Moses then presented himself to the king who was astonished and bade him speak the name of his God. On hearing it he fell down speechless, and one of the priests who dealt disparagingly with a tablet on which the sacred name was written, died with a convulsion (27.25f.). An account follows of the ten plagues, showing the writer's liking for the mysterious and the magical, all of which have the effect of glorifying Moses, the legendary hero of Israel.

Elsewhere he is described as God's 'Chosen One' (Lives of the Prophets 2.14), as a mild man whose anger is 'moderated by reason'

(IV Macc. 2.17) and as 'best of men' whom God had chosen to deliver his people from Egypt (Ezekiel the Tragedian, *Exagoge* 1.96). In this last-mentioned book interesting reference is made to a dream which comes to Moses and is interpreted by his father-in-law. In a scene somewhat reminiscent of the investiture scene in Daniel 7 he sees 'on Sinai's peak' 'what seemed a throne' on which sat 'a man of noble mien' with a sceptre in his hand. God – for such he is – beckons him to approach. The account continues:

> I made approach and stood before the throne,
> He handed o'er the sceptre and he bade
> me mount the throne, and gave to me the crown;
> then he himself withdrew from off the throne (ll. 73–76).

It is a sign that he will 'cause a mighty throne to rise' and that he will 'rule and govern men' (ll. 85f.). He has been chosen by God to be his grand-vizier.

(c) A legendary figure

Elsewhere in this same work further illustrations are given of the use of traditional or legendary material. For example, the land to which Moses flees is not Midian as in Exodus 2.15, but 'a land that bears Libya's name' (l. 60) where 'tribes of sundry races dwell throughout; the dark skinned Aethiops' (ll. 61f.). The name 'Libya', however, in antiquity does not refer to the country so called today, but rather to Africa as a whole, so that the reference here to 'sundry races' and 'Ethiopians' is quite in keeping. It was there that Moses is said to have married a woman named Sepphorah, thus bringing the story into line with the reference in Numbers 12.1 where it is said he took an Ethiopian woman as his wife. The historian Demetrius (in *Praeparatio Evengelica* 9.29) indicates that Sepphorah was indeed an Ethiopian, descended from Abraham through his son Keturah (Gen. 25.6).

A further legendary allusion is found in a graphic description of the phoenix, that mythical bird –

> full wondrous, such as man has never seen;
> 'twas near in scope to twice the eagle's size,
> with plumage iridescent, rainbow-hued (ll.255f.)

The significance of its appearance is not too obvious, but its association in the context with palm trees and springs of water may suggest some kind of paradisal connection.

The information given by Aristobulus is less extensive than that given by, say, Artapanus and less syncretistic in its emphasis. It too contains legendary material, though this is less marked. Moses is presented as the idealized man, not just in the eyes of his fellow-Hebrews, but in the eyes of pagan poets and philosophers as well. Aristobulus, for example, would have agreed with Artapanus that Moses was indeed a philosopher of the first order, for it was from the philosophy of the Hebrews that the Greeks had learned their first lessons (Fragment 3, title) and from the Law of Moses that philosophers like Plato and Pythagoras had borrowed, that Law having already been translated from Hebrew into Greek before the time of the Septuagint (*Praeparatio Evangelica* 13.12.1f.). Reference is made in fragment two to his wisdom and 'divine spirit' which caused people to marvel and to proclaim him as a prophet, for he was able to read the signs of nature and the signs of the times and to express himself 'in many ways' (8.10.3f.). The same themes are taken up in fragment four where Moses expounds 'the whole genesis of the world' in terms of the 'words of God' as revealed in the Law. In this he is followed by Pythagoras, Socrates and Plato in their contemplation of 'the arrangements of the universe'. What is more, writers and poets like Orpheus and Aratus express in their verses ideas similar to those of Moses himself (13.13.3–4,6). Another illustration of dependence by others on the Law of Moses is given in fragment five where it is said that Homer, Hesiod and Linus all demonstrate that the seventh day, in keeping with the Jewish teaching on the Sabbath, is holy and complete (13.12.13ff.).

This superiority of the Law over all other cultures is demonstrated also by the Palestinian writer Eupolemus who confirms the outstanding qualities of Moses (9.26.1). He describes him as 'the first wise man' just as Enoch and Abraham are described elsewhere. He it was, moreover, who 'first taught the alphabet to the Jews'; they in turn passed it on to the Phoenicians who taught it to the Greeks. The reference here is primarily to alphabetic writing in which the Phoenicians in particular took great pride, and may in addition signify literature and science in general (cf. Martin Hengel, *Judaism and Hellenism*, 1974, vol. 1, p.92). Moses is thus the author of both. Besides these things, it was he who 'first wrote laws for the Jews', the reference being to the Torah of God which, by implication, was the first of all books to be written. By so doing he demonstrated that, in the ranks of lawgivers, he was first among 'the wise' (9.26.1).

Pseudo-Philo adds his own touches of the legendary and the miraculous to his portrait of Moses. He tells, for example, how the spirit of God came upon Miriam one night, before Moses was born, and she saw a dream. In the dream an angel appeared telling her to report to her parents that the child to be born from them would be 'cast forth into the water' and that 'likewise through him the water (would) be dried up' and the people would be saved through him (9.10), thus foretelling his experience in the ark and his dividing of the Red Sea.

And as with his birth, so also with his death, the scenario is supernatural. His death will be an event in which 'all the angels will mourn' and 'the heavenly hosts will be saddened' (19.12). On that day the hymns of the angels will cease (19.16). Even 'the stars will hasten and the light of the sun will hurry to fall and the light of the moon will not remain' (19.13). But God himself will bury him 'with his own hands on a high place and in the light of all the world' (19.16). He will glorify him with his fathers and will raise him, together with his fathers, to dwell in 'the immortal dwelling place that is not subject to time' (19.12). In such high regard was Moses held that, compared with the day of his death, there was 'no such day from the one on which the Lord made man upon the earth, nor shall there be such for ever' (19.16).

(d) A mediator of revelation

The Book of Jubilees and the Testament of Moses, representing Palestinian Judaism, paint a different picture from that of, say, Artapanus and Aristobulus, representing as these latter do the Judaism of the Hellenistic world. The account of Israel's history set forth in Jubilees is in the form of a divine revelation given to Moses on Mount Sinai (Ex. 24.18) and recorded in writing by 'the angel of the presence' (1.27ff.). The account in the Testament of Moses takes the form of a disclosure by Moses to Joshua on Mount Nebo of events leading up to the time of the end. They are revelations that carry with them the divine *imprimatur*.

In the case of Jubilees 'the Lord revealed to (Moses) both what was in the beginning and what will occur (in the future), the account of the division of all the days of the Law and the testimony' (1.4). This revelation, which is to be written down in a book, is in the nature of a 'second law' corresponding to the 'first law' which is the Torah itself contained in the Pentateuch (cf. 6.22). In other words, what we have here in Jubilees is not simply a record of past events or a repetition of the Sinai events as recorded in the Book of Exodus; it is a utilization, supplementation and application of the biblical account so as to interpret its meaning and significance for the writer's contemporaries within the cultural and religious environment of their own day. Re-interpreted revelation was no less revelation and Moses was God's agent in mediating its truths to succeeding generations.

The writer of the Testament of Moses re-affirms that Moses was chosen by God to be the mediator of this revelation to his people and adds that it was not because of any strength he might have, but by reason of God's mercies (12.7); nevertheless, God's choice of him for this role had been in the divine mind from the very beginning – 'He did design and devise me, who was prepared from the beginning of the world, to be the mediator of his covenant' (1.14). It is unlikely that the notion of pre-existence or pre-creation is to be read into these words, but they single out Moses as one chosen by God for this special purpose, to make known the pre-existent Torah as God's supreme revelation.

The appearance of a fragment of a cryptic astrological document among the Dead Sea scrolls with the title 'Midrash of the words of Moses' reminds us of the part played by astrology (and astronomy) as a means of divine revelation and of the ambivalent attitude towards it adopted by Jewish writers of this time. Astrology, of course, had long and close association with Babylonia and Egypt, as we have seen, and had taken its place within the Hellenistic culture which influenced Jew and Gentile alike. An interesting allusion is made to the origins of this 'science' in Jubilees 8.2ff. which tells how Cainan, Noah's grandson, 'found a writing which the ancestors had engraved on stone' which he duly read and transcribed. Then the comment is added: 'And he sinned because of what was in it, since there was in it the teaching of the Watchers by which they used to observe the omens of the sun and moon and stars within all the signs of heaven'. Having copied it down, Cainan was afraid to tell Noah about it 'lest he be angry with him because of it'. This anti-astrological stance is evident in the Book of Jubilees (cf. also 12.16ff.; see p. 72) and in I Enoch (cf. 16.3; see p. 72), whereas a positive attitude is adopted in, say, the Treatise of Shem where much is made of the signs of the Zodiac and their influence on natural phenomena and human affairs. The reason for a negative attitude is perhaps to be found in Josephus who indicates that Cainan's father, Arpachsad, is the ancestor of the Chaldeans (*Ant.*

I.146) and so Cainan's discovery of the secret astrological writing is the origin of star worship with its emphasis on magic and omens. Secrets revealed in this way were a betrayal of the mysteries of God and came from fallen angels (I En.16.3). And so, in order to counter such revelations, tainted as they were, God gave fresh revelations to Enoch, Noah and Abraham concerning secret books, the course of the stars, the cure of ills and so forth. In the words of Martin Hengel, these writers 'wanted to set against the "demonic" Chaldean, Egyptian or Greek "wisdom" a more comprehensive, genuine wisdom of their own, encompassing the cosmos and history, and founded on revelation and not on betrayal' (op.cit., p.243). The ambivalence of the Jews in this regard, however, is quite marked, and the influence of astrology is noticeable even in the case of a conservative body like the Qumran covenanters among whose writings a number of fragments have been found, in addition to the one mentioned above, dealing sometimes in cryptic writing with esoteric astrological teachings. This is noticeable also, albeit in a transformed state, as we have seen, in the Enoch tradition as represented in I Enoch, and in the Moses tradition as represented by the Book of Jubilees.

(e) A perfect teacher

But not only is he the mediator of revelation, Moses is at the same time a supreme teacher of the divine law which is the content and substance of that revelation. The Testament of Moses describes him as 'that sacred spirit, worthy of the Lord, manifold and incomprehensible, master of leaders (or, master of the word), faithful in all things, the divine prophet for the whole earth, the perfect teacher' (11.16). To the writer of the Book of Jubilees also Moses is 'the perfect teacher'. Under this pseudonym he seeks to deepen piety and to encourage strict obedience to the Law by means of the observance of right ritual and sacred times and seasons. In so doing he makes use of the biblical narrative, but supplements it so as to strengthen his appeal to his contemporaries and to make his teaching more relevant to the apostate days in which he was then living.

In the time of Antiochus Epiphanes the Sabbath and festival days had been profaned, circumcision forbidden, sacrifices banned, books burned and nudity on the racing track encouraged. The Book of Jubilees, in the name of Moses, seeks to set the balance right by presenting again the claims of the Law which is both authoritative and eternal, tracing its origins back to Moses and beyond him to the patriarchs of old. And so in the story of Adam and Eve in the Garden a warning is given against nudity (3.26) which distinguishes the animals from man (3.30), laws are laid down concerning the purification of women after childbirth (3.8ff.), regulations are given regarding the giving of tithes and the ordering of sacrifices (32.1ff.), strict observance is enjoined of the Sabbath (2.17ff.) and of circumcision (15.24ff.). The Sabbath is described as 'a great sign' between God and his covenant people together with 'the angels of the presence and the angels of sanctification' (2.17f.), having been 'kept in heaven before it was made known on earth' (2.30). So too with circumcision, these very angels themselves were circumcized 'from the day of their creation' and so were able to share in the sacred festivals (15.27); it is indeed 'an eternal ordinance ordained and written in the heavenly tablets' (15.25).

And as with rites and ceremonies, so also with times and seasons. Particular days, alongside the Sabbath, were reckoned to be particularly holy and so it was of vital importance that these, and the religious festivals which fell on them, should be observed with careful and unchanging regularity. A calendar based on a lunar month and giving a year of 354 days was of no use for this purpose, for it resulted in festivals falling on different days in different years. To safeguard against such calamities the Book of Jubilees, as we have already noted, advocates (like the Covenanters of Qumran) a solar calendar of twelve thirty-day-months, giving a total of 360 days to which was added an intercalary day every three months, making a total of 364 days. By this means the regular safeguarding of festivals and holy days was guaranteed. Such festivals and holy days had been ordained from the beginning by God and had in fact been practised by the patriarchs of old (cf. 6.17f.; 32.4). Their antiquity and so authority is emphasized by the claim that they had their origin in divine revelation (32.21ff.) and had been passed on in the form of sacred books by the ancient patriarchs to Jacob and through Jacob to Levi and through Levi to his descendants (45.16). The writer of the Book of Jubilees – no doubt of priestly stock himself – was now making known in Moses' name these same traditions that he himself had received, declaring the 'signs of the covenant' and calling his people back to observance of the Law of God.

The picture of Moses that thus emerges is that of a 'perfect teacher' who is both prophet and priest declaring the eternal validity of the Law, observed by angels and practised by patriarchs of old.

(f) A prophet of future events

As we have already noted, according to the Book of Jubilees God revealed to Moses not only 'what was in the beginning', but also 'what will occur (in the future)' (1.4). In describing these future occurrences the author makes no reference to any great cataclysmic event such as is found in a number of apocalyptic writings of the time, nor is he concerned to describe in any detail the coming age of triumph and bliss to which others refer. On the contrary, the coming of the 'messianic kingdom' will be a gradual process in which heaven and earth will be renewed as God's people grow in spiritual awareness (1.29; 4.26; 23.26–28). The important thing is that, with the approach of these days, men will begin to study the laws of God and return to righteousness (23.26). Their lives will be lengthened and they will reach an age of a thousand years (23.27) with no Satan and no evil to hurt them (23.24). There will be no resurrection, for 'their bones will rest in the earth'; but 'their spirits will have much joy' (23.31). Judgment will fall on sinful men (4.24) and fallen angels (5.10); Mastema who had assisted the Egyptians (48.2ff.) and was the source of so much evil, will be destroyed (10.8; 23.29).

A description of the coming of this messianic kingdom is given also in the Testament of Moses where Moses outlines events from his lifetime onwards and foretells a time of apostasy after the return from exile, and the suffering of God's people that will ensue (2.1–8.5). This suffering is epitomized in a Levite named Taxo who, together with his seven sons, expresses his readiness to die in the sure belief that 'our blood will be avenged before the Lord' (9.7). Such suffering will precipitate the intervention of God: 'His kingdom will appear throughout his whole creation. Then the devil will have an end' (10.1). The Heavenly One will arise from his kingly throne, the earth will tremble, the sun will be darkened, the moon will be broken, the sea will retire, and 'the Eternal One will come to work vengeance on the nations' (10.3–7). The Gentiles will be destroyed together with their idols (10.7); the devil will be defeated and sorrow depart (10.1); Israel will be raised to 'the heaven of the stars' (10.9) where they will rejoice to see the lot of their enemies below (10.10). The picture thus presented is supramundane, with no resurrection and no earthly kingdom.

The account of Moses' own death, as recorded in Deut. 34, led to many speculations and the development of many legends in later literature, chiefly within the rabbinic tradition. In the New Testament,

Jude 9 records a dispute between Michael and Satan for the body of Moses, a story which may have come from a supposed lost ending of the Testament of Moses or from an Assumption of Moses now combined with the Testament and surviving only in part, or else from oral tradition. Josephus is apparently familiar with a belief in the bodily assumption of Moses: 'A cloud of a sudden descended upon him and he disappeared in a ravine. But he has written of himself in the sacred books that he died, for fear lest they should venture to say that by reason of his surpassing virtue he had gone back to the Deity' (*Ant*.IV. 326). This belief finds some corroboration in the Gospels where Moses appears alongside Enoch and Elijah, both of whom had been transported bodily to heaven (Mark 9.4f. and parallel passages). In view of the fact, however, that the Testament of Moses speaks plainly of the death of Moses (1.15; 10.12,14; 11.7,8), his assumption, to which reference is made in the Fathers, is presumably that of his soul and not his body.

In Pseudo-Philo Moses is presented not only as a great leader and encourager, but also as one to whom God makes known the secrets of his ways. This is demonstrated in such a passage as 19.10–16 where he is shown mysteries of the physical universe and the immortal dwelling place (10.12), where he and his fathers will dwell eternally. At that time God will visit the world, the days will be shortened, the sun and the moon will fail to give their light, and he will hasten to raise up those who are sleeping to 'dwell in the place of sanctification' (19.13). Come what may, however, God's covenant people will remain, for 'it is easier to take away the foundations and the topmost part of the earth and to extinguish the light of the sun and to darken the light of the moon than for anyone to uproot the planting of the Most Powerful or to destroy his vine' (18.10). Moses, to whom God has revealed 'the end of the world so that he might establish his statutes' (19.4), has no equal among men, for 'who will give us another shepherd like Moses or such a judge for the sons of Israel to pray always for our sins and to be heard for our iniquities' (19.3)?

3. Ezra, 'the second Moses'

Alongside the tradition of Moses as lawgiver and revealer there grew up another, associated with the name of Ezra, in which there is a marked degree of assimilation between the two figures and in which Ezra is presented as a 'second Moses'. This Ezra-tradition continued within the Christian church and is represented by a number of Christian writings among which are the Greek Apocalypse of Ezra, the Vision of Ezra, the Questions of Ezra, the Revelation of Ezra and the Apocalypse of Sedrach.

Of the greatest significance, however, is the apocalyptic writing, usually designated 'IV Ezra', dating from about AD 100. This Jewish work is to be found in chapters 3–14 of the book entitled 'II Esdras' in the Apocrypha. Chapters 1–2 and 15–16 are later Christian additions. As we shall see, the book consists of a series of visions granted to one, Salathiel, who is 'also called Ezra' (3.1). Whilst the picture of Ezra that emerges has something in common with the biblical character of that name, the differences are much more marked.

(a) The scribe

In scripture Ezra is presented as 'a ready scribe in the law of Moses' (Ezra 7.6) who 'set his heart to seek the law of the Lord and to do it' (Ezra 7.10). More than that, he 'read in the book, in the law of God, distinctly' and 'gave the sense, so that they understood the reading' (Neh. 8.8), i.e. Ezra the scribe makes available to the people of Israel the Law of Moses and interprets it in such a way that they are able to apply it to their daily lives, a task in which he is followed by the Sopherim and later on by the Rabbis.

Interesting comment is made on this process in IV Ezra 14 where reference is made to a revelation of the Torah granted to Ezra and alongside that of a secret (apocalyptic) tradition. It tells how Ezra is sitting under an oak tree when he hears God's voice calling to him out of a bush as in the case of Moses of old: 'I revealed myself in a bush and spoke to Moses when my people were in bondage in Egypt; and I sent him and led my people out of Egypt; and I led him up on Mount Sinai, where I kept him with me many days, and I told him many wondrous things, and showed him the secrets of the times and declared to him the end of the times. Then I commanded him, saying, These words you shall publish openly, and these you shall keep secret' (14.3–6). The meaning seems to be that God revealed to Moses on Sinai not only the Torah which was to be published openly, but also a 'secret' tradition which was to be kept hidden. This latter is presumably the apocalyptic tradition which records great crises in world history and the fast-approaching end.

The association of such a tradition with the name of Moses may be seen in such a book as the Testament of Moses, where Moses instructs

Joshua to 'preserve the books' he is now entrusting to his care: 'You shall arrange them, anoint them with (oil of) cedar, and deposit them in earthenware jars in the place which (God) has chosen from the beginning of the creation of the world' (1.17). These hidden books are to be preserved until 'the day of recompense' when the Lord will visit them 'in the consummation of the end of days' (1.18). So too in the Book of Jubilees where Moses is bidden to record all the events of history, what is past and what is yet to come: 'Write down for yourself all of the matters which I shall make known to you on this mountain: What (was) in the beginning and what (will be) at the end . . . until I shall descend and dwell with them in all the ages of eternity' (1.26). The message of such passages seems to be that Moses is the author of both Torah and a secret tradition whose secrets are to be made known at the time of the end.

But, according to Jewish tradition, the record of Moses' revelation on Sinai had been destroyed by fire when Nebuchadnezzar captured Jerusalem in 587 BC. Thus we read in IV Ezra: 'Your Law has been burned, and so no one knows the things which have been done or will be done' (14.21). The implication of these words seems to be that the fire destroyed not only the 'open' books of the Law, but the 'secret' books as well.

Ezra now offers to take Moses' place, as it were, and to write 'everything that has happened in the world from the beginning, the things which were written in your Law' (14.22) and asks for the inspiration of the Holy Spirit to enable him in his task. In answer to his prayer, God gives him a cup 'full of something like water, but its colour was like fire' (14.39f.). He takes it and drinks, and thereupon his wisdom is increased, his memory sharpened and his mouth opened (14.40f.). Like Moses, he sets aside forty days to receive and record what God will reveal to him. He dictates what he has heard to five scribes who record the revelation in ninety-four books (14.44). At the end of that time God again speaks: 'Make public the twenty-four books that you wrote first, and let the worthy and the unworthy read them; but keep the seventy that were written last, in order to give them to the wise among your people. For in them is the spring of understanding, the fountain of wisdom and the river of knowledge' (14.45ff.). The twenty-four books that are to be published openly are obviously those of canonical scripture, and the seventy books that are to be kept secret are presumably the apocalyptic writings to which IV Ezra itself belongs. The number 'seventy' used in this connection may be symbolic, representing something that is comprehensive. Or, it may be more subtle in its reference than this. The word 'secret' (*swd*, pronounced sōd), which occurs several times in this context, has in Hebrew a numerical value of 'seventy' (s = 60, w = 6, d = 4), a factor which may have influenced the writer's use of this particular number.

Be that as it may, Ezra the scribe who makes known the Law of God is now presented as Ezra the seer who by divine revelation declares the denouement of history, the coming of the messianic kingdom and the mysteries of the life to come.

(b) The seer

The reader of IV Ezra looks in vain for any single theme running through the book. Rather, it consists of a medley of ideas which may reflect diverse authorship or, more likely, confused and confusing traditions prevailing at that time. It takes the form of seven visions given by God to Ezra in Babylon in which the latter shows great concern over God's dealings with Israel and engages in speculation concerning the coming kingdom, the world to come and the fate of men and nations.

In the first vision (3.1–5.19) the seer is puzzled and grieved that a righteous God should allow his people to suffer in the way they do, but is assured by Uriel that the end of this present age is near at hand. There are evident signs that that hour is fast approaching. In the second vision (5.20–6.34) the same theme is pursued, with an additional query about the lot of those who die before the new age is ushered in. In the third vision (6.35–9.25) reference is made to the final judgment and its effect on the righteous and the wicked. The new Jerusalem will appear and the Messiah will rule for 400 years at the close of which he and those who are with him will die. After a silence lasting seven days will come the resurrection, the judgment and the revealing of Gehenna and Paradise when few will be saved. In the fourth vision (9.26–10.59) a mourning woman appears representing the devastated city of Zion. Quite suddenly she disappears and in her place stands the new Jerusalem. In the fifth vision (11.1–12.39) a re-interpretation is given of the vision in Daniel 7. Under the symbolism of an eagle with twelve wings and three heads, the seer depicts the Roman Empire and the coming of the Messiah who, under the figure of a lion, destroys it and delivers the righteous. In the sixth vision (13.1–58) the Messiah appears as a transcendent figure – a man rising from the sea and flying with the clouds of heaven who destroys his enemies with fire from his mouth and delivers the righteous. In the seventh vision (14.1–48) the account is given of the revelation and writing of the ninety-four books and assurance offered to the seer: 'You shall be taken up from among men, and henceforth you shall live with my Son . . . until the times are ended. For the age has lost its youth, and the times begin to grow old' (14.9f.).

It will be clear from this brief sketch of Ezra's visions that theological consistency is not the most obvious mark of this work! The messianic kingdom is a cherished goal to which the writer looks forward, but it is to be of a purely temporary nature; the Messiah appears as a mortal man who will reign for 400 years and then die as others do, but elsewhere he is represented as a transcendent figure, pre-existent and powerful; his burning desire is that his own people will be saved and the Gentiles destroyed, but he laments with the whole human race at the judgment and torment that will befall them; that judgment expresses itself in the individual destiny and the moral dichotomy of Gehenna and Paradise, but it can take the form of political recrimination against a foreign power; the resurrection is for the righteous only, but elsewhere it is a resurrection of *all* men, albeit for judgment. Only one thing is certain: the consummation of all things is in the hands of God and the end is near.

(c) The critic

The first vision, we are told, came 'in the thirtieth year after the destruction of our city' (3.1). This no doubt has a double reference – the fall of Jerusalem in 587 BC and again in AD 70; and the agitation felt by the biblical Ezra reflects that of the author himself. The reason for his agitation is the sight he sees of 'the desolation of Zion and the wealth of those who lived in Babylon' (4.2) – God actually endures those who sin and spares those who act wickedly, but has destroyed his own people (3.30): 'I have travelled widely among the nations and have seen that they abound in wealth though they are unmindful of your commandments' (3.33). His thoughts 'well up in his heart' and he demands to know 'why Israel has been given over to the Gentiles as a reproach, why the people whom (God) loved had been given to godless tribes' (4.23). 'It would be better for us not to be here than to come here . . . and to suffer and not understand why' (4.12). The 'four-footed beasts' are better off than human beings, for at least 'they do not look for a judgment, nor do they know of any torment or salvation promised to them after death' (7.66). God had graciously

111

chosen Israel and given to his people his Law (3.19f; 9.31f.), and though it had been offered also to the Gentiles they had scorned it and denied his covenants (7.24). Why, then, this apparent denial by God of his just dealings with Israel? After all, God is responsible for the creation of mankind and the calling of his chosen people. Why should things be as they are? The answer of Uriel, in God's name, is typical of the book as a whole – the ways of God are inscrutable: 'Your understanding has utterly failed regarding this world, and do you think you can comprehend the way of the Most High?' (4.2) If Ezra can weigh the fire or measure the wind or call back yesterday, then he will show him the way he desires to see (4.4f.)!

This problem of Israel's suffering is closely related to another – the problem of human sinfulness and the apparent incorrigible wickedness of the human heart. The sin of Adam was not his alone (see pp. 20f.); it had affected all those who were his descendants. The seer's problem, therefore, is not just the suffering of his own people, but also the awful plight of all mankind. As he contemplates the terrible punishment that awaits them by reason of their sin, he laments aloud their tragic fate in the world to come and intercedes passionately on their behalf. Having appealed to the divine justice, he now in a memorable passage appeals to God's mercy: 'I know, my lord, that the Most High is now called merciful, because he has mercy on those who have not yet come into the world; and gracious, because he is gracious to those who turn in repentance to his law; and patient, because he shows patience toward those who have sinned, since they are his own works; and bountiful, because he would rather give than take away; and abundant in compassion, because he makes his compassions abound more and more to those now living and to those who are gone and to those yet to come' (7.132–136). He awaits a reply which, when it comes, gives cold comfort indeed: 'Many have been created, but few will be saved' (8.3). Ezra the critic receives no other answer to his plea.

The picture of Ezra thus presented in this writing, whilst having something in common with the biblical Ezra in the account given of the re-publishing of the Torah of Moses, has wandered far away from its prototype and assumed shapes and colours determined by the hopes and fears of the writer himself and by the varied traditions prevalent in his day. Not only is it different; in places – as in its universal plea on behalf of the wicked – it even contradicts the narrow nationalism of Ezra of old.

IX

Prophets and Portents

1. The sources

References to the prophets are found scattered throughout the pseude-pigraphical writings some of which claim, under the guise of pseudon-ymity, to have been written by them or under their inspiration. The most comprehensive and inclusive in this regard is the Lives of the Prophets (which is not really a pseudepigraphon in the strict sense of that word), written probably in Palestine in the early part of the first century AD. It is a Jewish writing, but shows Christian influence, having been preserved and passed on largely within the Christian tradition. As its preface indicates, it records 'the names of the prophets, and where they are from, and where they died and how, and where they lie'. As such it shows great interest in the deaths of the prophets and their burial places which are held in high honour and are marked by appropriate monuments which are objects of veneration.

The 'atmosphere' of this book is very different from those canonical prophetic books which bear the names and contain the oracles of the prophets here described. The strong moral condemnation of Israel's sin so often heard there gives way in the Lives of the Prophets to legendary tales, miraculous events and prognostications of the future by means of strange portents in heaven and on earth; moral pronounce-ments are replaced by intercessory prayer; Beliar, called 'the serpent' (12.13), is held responsible for evil on the earth; martyrdom is extolled and resurrection assured.

The 'information' given there concerning the prophet Isaiah is supplemented by the so-called Ascension of Isaiah. This is a composite work within which three separate writings can be detected: the Martyrdom of Isaiah (1.1–3.12 and 5.1–16), the Testament of

113

Hezekiah (3.13–4.22) and the Vision of Isaiah (6.1–11.43). The first of these (first century AD, based on traditions of the early second century BC) tells the story of Isaiah's death at the hands of Manasseh; the second (about the close of the first century AD) is a Christian interpolation, giving an account of a vision received by Isaiah just prior to his death; and the third (possibly the second century AD) is also Christian in origin, consisting of a vision in which Isaiah is transported through the seven heavens where he witnesses the descent and then the ascent of the Lord.

Several writings of the period contribute to our understanding of the changed and changing picture of the prophet Jeremiah. II Baruch, or the Syriac Apocalypse of Baruch as it is sometimes called, was probably written early on in the second century AD and purports to be the work of Jeremiah's secretary, Baruch, in the years following the destruction of Jerusalem in 587 BC. Somewhat more light is cast on the character of Jeremiah by the Paraleipomena ('things omitted') of Jeremiah which also goes by the name IV Baruch; it is to be dated probably fairly early on in the second century AD and may, in its present form, be dependent on II Baruch; it is basically a Jewish document, but shows evidence of Christian interpolation. In the Greek version of the work it is attributed to Jeremiah, and in the Ethiopic version to Baruch; hence the double designation. The History of the Rechabites (first to fourth century AD is, for the most part, an imaginary 'filling out' of the account given in Jeremiah 35 concerning the fidelity of the Rechabites. It shows marked Christian traits, but no doubt reflects Jewish traditions even prior to the second century AD. Its story concerning the visit of one, Zosimus, to 'the island of the Blessed Ones' tells how the Rechabites, for such they are, journey there in the time of Jeremiah the prophet.

The minor prophets are represented by the Apocalypse of Zephaniah (first century BC to first century AD), an account in the first person of the seer's journey through the heavenly regions in company with an angelic guide. The theme of judgment features prominently in which the angels escort the souls of the ungodly through the gates of Hades to their eternal punishment. It is not clear why the seer, in writing this book, adopted the name of Zephaniah, although there are some parallels with that biblical prophet; the angelic dialogues described in the apocalypse have more in common with the prophet Zechariah.

The Apocalypse of Elijah, despite its name, has very little if anything to do with that prophet. He is in fact mentioned only twice in the text, each time in association with Enoch (4.7; 5.32) and for this reason his name may have come to be used in the title. It is a composite work, showing clear Christian influence, but probably containing earlier Jewish material. The date is difficult to define, but may be given as from the first to the fourth centuries AD. Despite its title, moreover, its actual form is hardly that of an apocalypse, although in content it relates to 'the end time' and has much to say concerning the Antichrist.

2. The lives of the prophets

In the Lives of the Prophets the writer gives brief cameos which are recognizable as portraits of Old Testament saints and heroes; but the differences are more marked than the similarities. The pictures presented introduce details which are either absent from the corresponding biblical account or else receive much less attention. Stress now comes to be laid on legend, miracle, portent and prayer, embracing Jewish traditions which, in the case of some at any rate, may go back over many years. It will be convenient to look here at the information given by the Lives and to supplement this, where available, with other material from the intertestamental years.

(a) The major prophets

The account given of the prophet Isaiah begins by stating that he died under Manasseh by being sawn in two (1.1). This ties in with the reference in Hebrews 11.37 which states concerning the early martyrs that 'they were stoned, they were sawn in two, they were killed with the sword' and indicates in all probability that this legend concerning Isaiah was known in pre-Christian times. It finds corroboration also in the Ascension of Isaiah where it says that 'Beliar was angry with Isaiah, and he dwelt in the heart of Manasseh, and he sawed Isaiah in half with a wood saw' (5.1, i.e. a saw for sawing wood, not 'a wooden saw'). No indication is given in the Old Testament as to how Isaiah met his death, but the writers of the Lives and the Ascension are alluding to a tradition which appears in fuller form in the Babylonian and Jerusalem Talmuds. In the former, Isaiah, as a punishment for saying he dwelt among a people of unclean lips (Isa. 6.5), was swallowed up by a cedar which was taken and sawn in half, thus bringing about his death. The same Talmud refers elsewhere to the fact that he was slain by Manasseh. A variation on this theme is given in the Jerusalem Talmud: there Isaiah is fleeing from Manasseh and hides in a cedar tree, but the fringes of his cloak are seen and he is discovered. Further details concerning the circumstances of Isaiah's death are given in the Ascension: while the prophet was being sawn asunder, a certain Samaritan named Belkira (2.12), who had acted as his accuser and as such was the agent of Beliar (5.4–9), stood by laughing and tempting him to say what he (and Beliar) would tell him, with their guarantee that Manasseh, the princes, the people and all Jerusalem would worship him (5.8). Isaiah refuses and is put to death.

Having alluded to the legend of Isaiah's death, the writer of the Lives refers to 'the miracle of Siloam' which God worked 'for the prophet's sake' (1.2). In answer to his prayer water came forth in the time before Hezekiah made the cisterns and the pools (1.3), so that the people in the city of Jerusalem, though besieged, were able to drink. The miraculous thing was that, when the Jews came, 'water would come out, but if foreigners (approached), (it would) not' (1.6). When Isaiah died he was buried nearby so that, even after his death, through his prayers, 'they might enjoy the benefit of the water' (1.8). It is clear that, both here and also in Josephus (*War* V.140), Siloam was regarded as a spring and not a pool. Three times over in these few verses (1.2,3,8) reference is made to the efficacy of Isaiah's prayers – an emphasis which, as we shall see, is evident throughout this and other related books.

Just as Hebrews 11.37 finds an echo in the cutting asunder of Isaiah, so it does also in the reported death of Jeremiah who, according to the Lives of the Prophets, was 'stoned by his people' (2.1). This finds support in IV Baruch 9 which, in its present form, represents a Christian redaction. It tells how, following a vision vouchsafed to Jeremiah, the people plot to stone him. Baruch and Abimelech (Ebed-melek of the biblical story, cf. Jer. 38.7–13) are grieved, but Jeremiah assures them he will not die before he has described all the mysteries he has seen. He tells them to bring a stone which he sets up. He then prays that God will make it take on the appearance of Jeremiah himself: 'and they were stoning the stone, thinking that it was Jeremiah' (9.28). The stone then cried out saying how stupid the people were to do such a thing and pointing out that Jeremiah stood in their midst. 'And when they saw him, they immediately ran at him with many stones, and his stewardship was fulfilled' (9.31).

In the Lives of the Prophets, moreover, it is reported that, before the capture of the Temple in Jerusalem, Jeremiah 'seized the ark of the Law and the things in it, and made them to be swallowed up in a rock' (2.11f.; cf. II Macc. 2.4ff.; Eupolemus in *Praeparatio Evangelica* 9.39.2–5); no one would bring it out except Aaron, and no one would open the tablets in it except Moses (2.14). A variation on this is recorded in II Baruch 6.5ff. which tells how an angel descends from heaven to the Holy of Holies and 'took from there the veil, the holy ephod, the mercy seat, the two tables, the holy raiment of the priests, the altar of incense, the forty-eight precious stones with which the priests were clothed, and all the holy vessels of the tabernacle'. With a loud voice he commanded the earth to receive them and 'guard them until the last times . . . And the earth opened its mouth and swallowed them up' (6.8f.). In the same book, however, use is made of another tradition still, in which a new Temple in a new city will appear on earth, prepared beforehand like Paradise (4.1ff.) and presumably with no need of the old vessels of Solomon's Temple. The evidence of IV Baruch agrees with that of the Lives: Jeremiah asks God what he must do with the vessels and is told to 'deliver them to the earth'. There they will remain safe until the time appointed (3.9–11,18). An elaboration of the account is given in the Lives of the Prophets which tells how, in the rock where the ark was concealed, the prophet 'set as a seal the name of God and the impression was like a carving made with iron, and a cloud covered the name, and no one knows the place nor is able to read the name to this day and to the consummation' (2.16). There, in the wilderness, 'between the two mountains on which Moses and Aaron lie' (2.17) the glory of God will never cease from the Law (2.18). Indeed, 'in the resurrection, the ark will be the first to be raised and will come out of the rock and be placed on Mount Sinai, and all the saints will be gathered to it' (2.15).

The legendary and miraculous character of the Lives of the Prophets is further illustrated in the qualities said to be possessed by Jeremiah both in his life and in his death. Such was the power of his prayers, for example, that by their means the Egyptians were rid of asps that had troubled them, together with 'the monsters of the waters, which the Egyptians called Nephoth and the Greeks crocodiles' (2.3). Following the example of Jeremiah, 'the faithful pray at the place every day' (2.4). Such was his influence even in death that the dust taken from his burial place had the power to cure asps' bites (2.4). So impressed indeed was Alexander the Macedonian that he transferred Jeremiah's remains to Alexandria and scattered them in a circle round the city so that the asps were kept away from the land, and the crocodiles from the river (2.5f.).

117

Another legendary tale appears in IV Baruch concerning the Ethiopian, Abimelech, whom Jeremiah wished to reward for his help by sparing him the sight of the desolated city of Jerusalem (3.13). Taking the Lord's advice, Jeremiah sent him to 'the farm of Agrippa' to gather a few figs to give to the sick among the people (3.21f.). In his absence the city was besieged and Jeremiah was taken off to Babylon (4.6). Meanwhile, Abimelech, carrying the figs, sat down to rest under a tree – and slept on for sixty-six years (5.2)! Imagining he had had only a short nap, he returned to Jerusalem, only to be utterly bewildered, for he recognized no one and the place had completely changed. On enquiring of an old man about Jeremiah, he is told the prophet is in Babylon. He meets Baruch and together they at the same time weep and rejoice. Seeing the figs in the basket, still fresh after sixty-six years, Baruch assures Abimelech: 'He who preserved the basket of figs, the same one again will preserve you by his power' (6.10). The preservation of Abimelech and the figs is a proof of the resurrection: 'The Mighty One is coming and will raise you in your tabernacle . . . Look at this basket of figs . . . they have not withered nor do they stink, but they are dripping with milk. Thus it will be for you, my flesh' (6.8f.).

They wish to communicate with Jeremiah in Babylon and so an angel bids them write a letter and send it by means of an eagle which conversed with a human voice (6.15ff.). Taking the letter and fifteen figs, the eagle flies to Babylon and waits for Jeremiah who comes out to bury a dead man. The eagle descends on the corpse and the man comes alive! Jeremiah reads the letter and sends one back by the eagle, counselling the people to be diligent in prayer (7.24,32; 9.3). Taking the figs, Jeremiah distributes them among the sick of the people (7.1–33).

We observe that, quite apart from such legendary stories, there are differences between the canonical book of Jeremiah and, say, II and IV Baruch. This is perhaps most noticeable in the place of exile to which Jeremiah is taken. Whereas in the biblical account he goes down into Egypt (Jer. 43.6f.), in both II Baruch (10.2f.; 33.2) and IV Baruch (3.15; 4.6; 5.19) he is taken to Babylon.

It is clear that, besides being recognized as a man of prayer, Jeremiah was regarded by each of these writers as a truly saintly man, greatly admired and greatly respected. Thus, in the Lives of the Prophets he is described as one on whom God had bestowed his favour 'so that he might become a partner of Moses, and they are together (presumably in heaven) to this day' (2.19). According to II Baruch he is one 'whose heart was found to be pure from sin' (9.1). In IV Baruch he is respectfully addressed as 'father' by Baruch (2.4,7) and by Abimelech (5.5,22) and several times over as God's 'chosen one' (1.6; 3.5; 7.16). The writer of the History of the Rechabites also holds him in high regard: not only did Jeremiah identify himself with the people in their grief at the fall of Jerusalem, 'he showed the common folk the way of goodness, and urged them to return to the Lord' (8.2).

The third major prophet, Ezekiel, is described by the writer of the Lives in somewhat similar legendary and miraculous language. It is possible that the manner of his death here recorded may again recall the reference in Hebrews 11.37 where it speaks of those who were 'slain by the sword'. It is stated simply that 'the ruler of the people Israel (presumably in Babylon) killed him' (3.2) as he was reproving him for the worship of idols. Further light may be cast on this incident by the representations of Ezekiel which appear on the north wall of the Dura Synagogue (AD 245) which indicate the arrest of that prophet by a dignitary and his subsequent beheading (cf. E. R. Goodenough, *Jewish Symbols in the Greco-Roman Period*, vol. 10, pp. 188–190; quoted in J. H. Charlesworth (ed), *The Old Testament Pseudepigrapha*, vol. 2, p. 388).

During his time in Babylon Ezekiel gave portents of the future and worked miracles among the people. One such portent concerned 'the river Chebar': when its waters failed, that was a sign of desolation; when it flooded, that was a sign that they would return to Jerusalem (3.5). This portent is coupled with a miracle which he performed when the Babylonians, afraid that the Israelites would rebel, came against them. But, as Moses had done at the Red Sea, Ezekiel now does at the Chebar: he makes the waters stop so that his people escape to the other side, but their enemies are drowned (3.6–9). One recension says that the miracle actually took place after Ezekiel's death for the benefit of the pilgrims who were on their way to pray at the prophet's grave.

Like Jeremiah, he too was a man of prayer: he made it a practice to pray for many who were at the point of death that they might be restored, and on one occasion, it is recorded, 'through prayer he furnished (the people) of his own accord with an abundant supply of fish' (3.10). Later legends went further still and indicated that he actually restored dead people to life again.

He was a great encourager of his people, giving them fresh hope for this life and the life to come by means of his portrayal of 'the valley of dry bones' which came alive again, and at the same time terrified the enemy by unspecified prodigies (3.11f.). One wonder he performed whilst in Babylon was 'to show the people Israel what was happening in Jerusalem and in the Temple' (3.13). It is recorded that on one occasion he was 'snatched up from there and went to Jerusalem to rebuke those who were faithless' (3.14) where he 'saw the pattern of the Temple' as Moses had done and as Daniel forecast it would be (3.15).

When in Babylon he pronounced judgment on the tribes of Dan and Gad because they persecuted those who observed the Law. In this connection he wrought a 'great wonder' by arranging that snakes devour their infants and their flocks and by foretelling that they would not return to their own land. He met frequent opposition from them and, in the end, died at the hands of one of their number (3.16–19).

(b) The minor prophets

The writer of the Lives gives a brief sketch of each of the twelve 'minor prophets' to which he adds a somewhat longer section on Daniel (see above, p. 53). Once more the legendary character of the accounts is in evidence. Of Hosea it is said that he gave a portent that 'the Lord would arrive upon the earth' if ever the oak tree at Shiloh were to divide into several trees. This came to pass when twelve oak trees sprouted from it (5.2). Micah is said to have been killed by Joram, Ahab's son, 'at a cliff' which perhaps should read 'by hanging' or 'by crucifixion' (6.2). Little is said about Amos, except that he was tortured cruelly by Amaziah whose son killed him with a club by striking him on the temple (another later tradition says he was killed by Uzziah who struck him on the forehead with a red-hot iron). Obadiah is described as a disciple of Elijah and 'the third captain of fifty' (II Kings 1.13) whom Elijah spared (9.3). Jonah is presented as the son of the widow of Zarephath (10.5ff.; cf. I Kings 17.8–16) whom Elijah raised to life again (10.6). He it was who gave a double portent: 'whenever they should see a stone crying out piteously, the end was at hand; and whenever they should see all the gentiles in Jerusalem, the entire city would be razed to the ground' (10.10f.). A portent was given too by Nahum, in this case concerning Nineveh, 'that it would be destroyed by fresh water and an underground fire' (11.2f.), which actually came to pass, for 'the lake which surrounds it inundated it during an earthquake, and the fire coming from the wilderness burned its higher section' (11.3).

The account given of Habakkuk repeats the story told in Bel and the Dragon (vv. 34–39) and tells how he was 'ministering to those who were harvesting his field'. Taking food with him, he told the members of his family he was going to a far country and bade them give the harvesters food if he was delayed. He departed for Babylon where he gave the meal to Daniel, and returning to his own harvesters as they were eating, he told no one what had happened, though he knew the people would soon return from Babylon (12.5–9). With these things in mind he gave his people a portent: they would see a light in the Temple, reminding them of its glory. But its end was near: 'by a western nation it will happen'. 'The curtain separating off the Holy of Holies will be torn into small pieces, and the capitals of the two pillars will be taken away and no one will know where they are; and they will be carried away by angels into the wilderness' (12.12). By this means 'the Lord will be recognized at the end' and 'those who are being pursued by the serpent' will be illumined (12.13).

Portents are likewise attributed to the prophet Zechariah (ch. 15) who is frequently confused with Zechariah the priest (ch.23; cf. II Chron. 24.20ff.). It is said that he prophesied the birth of sons to Jozadak and Shealtiel and also forecast the victory of Cyrus whom he praised and blessed (15.3f.). At the same time, on the basis of visions he had received, he prophesied concerning 'the end of the Gentiles, Israel, the Temple and the laziness of prophets and priests' (15.5). The prophet Malachi was honoured by the whole people as 'holy and gentle'; his name, meaning 'angel', was most appropriate 'for he was indeed beautiful to behold' (16.1f.). Whatever he said in prophecy, on the same day an angel appeared and confirmed it (16.3). While still a young man he died.

About the prophet Zephaniah little is said in the Lives, but this is compensated for in the Apocalypse that bears his name. The text is very far from being complete, but the picture that comes over is that of a man gentle in spirit and earnest in prayer who, together with saints and angels, intercedes regularly for those who are in torment (2.8f.; 8.4; 11.1ff.; 11.5ff.). God will be compassionate (2.9) and give opportunity for repentance (10.10), but the wrath of God is not to be gainsaid (12.5). The prophet himself is immune from the torments that afflict the wicked, for he has triumphed over the accuser and has prevailed (9.1ff.). Being thus assured, he puts on 'an angelic garment' and joins the ranks of the angels whose language he understands and unites his voice with theirs in prayer (8.1–4).

(c) Earlier prophets

In Numbers 11.26–29 reference is made to two prophets, Eldad and Medad (or Modad) who were numbered among the seventy elders appointed to assist Moses, but who, unlike the others, remained 'within the camp' and were criticized by Joshua for prophesying there. No mention is made of the content of their prophecies. This, however, is compensated for in a pseudepigraphon which was known in rabbinic circles and in the early church. The only surviving quotation from it is a brief reference in the Shepherd of Hermas which reads: ' "The Lord is near to those who turn (to him)", as it is written in the (book of) Eldad and Modad who prophesied in the desert to the people' (Vision 2.3.4). Some indication of its contents may be gleaned from the Targum of Pseudo-Jonathan on Numbers 11.26 which suggests an assault on Jerusalem involving Gog and Magog, and the defeat of evil by intervention of the Messiah at the time of the end. The existence of such a book illustrates the tendency, recognizable elsewhere also, to fill in the gaps in the biblical records in terms of the hopes and beliefs current at the time of writing.

In the Lives of the Prophets, following reference to the minor prophets, the writer describes in brief the exploits of Nathan, Ahijah, Joad, Azariah, Elijah, Elisha and finally Zechariah son of Jehoiada the priest. Nathan, it is said, foresaw David's transgression with Bathsheba and hastened to warn him. Unfortunately, Beliar hindered him, for on the way he found the naked body of a murdered man by the roadside and was delayed, arriving too late to warn David of what would take place. He could only return home weeping (17.1ff.). Very little is said about Joad who is the un-named prophet mentioned in I Kings 13.1–32. Here again we have a case of later tradition filling in details, in this case supplying him with a name which in fact appears with variations in different traditions. In Josephus, for example, he is called Jadon (*Ant.* VIII.231) and in the rabbinic tradition he is identified with the seer Iddo mentioned in II Chronicles 9.29. Elijah's birth, it is said, was marked by a miraculous sign, for when he was about to be born 'his father Sobacha saw that men of shining white appearance were greeting him and wrapping him in fire, and they gave him flames of fire to eat' (21.2). This was a portent, for when he reported it in Jerusalem, 'the oracle' informed him of its meaning: 'Do not be afraid, for his dwelling will be light and his word judgment, and he will judge Israel' (21.3). (Elsewhere, in the Apocalypse of

Elijah 4.7–19, mention is made of Elijah's martyrdom, together with that of Enoch; but this is in all probability a Christian passage influenced by the martyrdom of the two witnesses in Rev. 11.1–12). Elisha's birth was also marked by 'a marvel', though less spectacular than that of Elijah: on that occasion 'the golden calf bellowed shrilly so that it was heard in Jerusalem' (22.2). This took place in Gilgal and confirms the belief expressed in some of the Church Fathers that one of Jeroboam's two golden calves was set up there and the other in Dan (22.2). As a result of this 'marvel' the priest, by means of the sacred lot Urim, declared that 'a prophet had been born to Israel who would destroy their carved images and molten idols' (22.2). Finally, reference is made to Zechariah the priest whom king Joash killed 'near the altar' and shed his blood 'in front of the Temple porch' (23.1). This same tradition is reflected in the Gospels where Jesus is reported as saying that Zechariah died 'between the sanctuary and the altar' (Matt. 23.35; Luke 11.51). From that time onwards 'visible portents appeared in the Temple': as a punishment from God 'the priests were not able to see a vision of angels of God or to give oracles from the Holy of Holies, or to enquire of the Ephod, or to answer the people through Urim as formerly' (23.2). Nothing is known of the giving of oracles through the Holy of Holies, but the Ephod and the Urim are well attested as vehicles of priestly pronouncements.

3. Two eschatological prophets

It is clear from various sources in the intertestamental period as well as from the New Testament itself that at that time the expectation ran high that, in the days of the approaching end, a prophet or prophets would arise who would prepare the people for the coming of the messianic age soon to dawn. This can be seen in such a passage as I Maccabees 4.46 where it is said that the stones of the altar of burnt offering which had been defiled by Antiochus Epiphanes should be 'stored in a convenient place in the temple hill until there should come a prophet to tell what to do with them'. And later on it is stated: 'The Jews and their priests decided that Simon should be their leader and high priest for ever, until a trustworthy prophet should arise' (14.41). In a day when it was believed that prophecy had ceased (see above, p. 9), they cherished the hope that the gift of prophecy might yet be revived, a hope which found focus in a great prophet who would arise at the time of the end and who would prepare the way for the coming kingdom. Within the pseudepigrapha, reference to such a prophet is very rare, as in the Testament of Benjamin 9.2 where it is said that the Temple of God will be replaced by a more glorious Temple and 'the twelve tribes shall be gathered there and all the nations, until such time as the Most High shall send forth his salvation through the ministration of the unique prophet'.

Such expectation of 'an eschatological prophet' found expression primarily in two Old Testament figures – in Elijah whose appearing was foretold in scripture 'before the great and terrible day of the Lord comes' (Mal. 4.5), and in Moses who had promised that God would raise up a prophet like himself who would speak all that God commanded (Deut. 18.15,18) – and features in both Jewish and Christian traditions.

(a) Elijah the forerunner

It is not surprising that considerable speculation should have surrounded the figure of Elijah and that in this he should have come to be closely associated with Enoch, having in mind that these two men, alone of all the biblical heroes, were translated to heaven and did not see death. But Elijah became the subject of speculation for a second reason. In Malachi 4.5f. we read: 'Behold, I will send you Elijah the prophet before the great and terrible day of the Lord comes. And he will turn the hearts of the fathers to their children and the hearts of children to their fathers, lest I come and smite the land with a curse'. Ben Sira echoes this expectation and sings Elijah's praises: not only will he 'calm the wrath of God' and 'turn the heart of the father to the son', he will also 'restore the tribes of Jacob' (48.10). That is, he is a great messianic figure who will appear at the last times and prepare the way for God and his kingdom to be established on earth. This belief continued to be upheld in later years within the rabbinic tradition. Within the Gospels it is reported that there were some who regarded Jesus as Elijah, even though he made no such claim for himself (Mark 11.28 and parallels).

Elsewhere, however, Elijah is thought of not as the promised Messiah who would deliver his people, but rather as the precursor or forerunner of the Messiah. This is suggested, for example, in I Enoch 90.31 where reference is made to Elijah under the symbolism of a ram which had been saved from its enemies and taken up to heaven to be with Enoch (89.52). There, in company with three angels who had escorted him and in the presence of Enoch, he is taken down to earth where he witnesses the events leading up to the judgment and the appearance of the Messiah himself, symbolized by 'a snow-white bull with huge horns' (90.37). It is clear from the Gospel records that such a tradition was deeply embedded in Jewish lore by the time of Jesus' public ministry and that Elijah's identification with John the Baptist came to be made by some (Luke 3.15; John 1.20). It is possible, moreover, that the Qumran Covenanters thought of their 'Teacher of Righteousness' as a forerunner of the Messiah in somewhat the same way as others thought of Elijah, but there is no evidence that they in fact identified him with that prophet.

The probability is that, in the earlier stages of the expectation, the hope was expressed not so much in the return of Elijah as such, but rather in the coming of an eschatological prophet who would be imbued with 'the spirit and power of Elijah' (Luke 1.17), as in the case of John the Baptist. In due course, however, the belief developed that Elijah, who had been taken up into heaven by God, would return from there to earth as herald of the Messiah and the messianic kingdom. It is extremely difficult, on the evidence available, to determine at what point such a belief in Elijah, as a heavenly visitor, came to make itself felt. James D. G. Dunn, having examined the sources, comes to the conclusion that '*there is in the period prior to the end of the first century* AD *no clear or firm evidence of a belief in the coming of Elijah or Enoch as a coming of the translated prophet or patriarch himself from heaven*' (*Christology in the Making*, 1980, p.94, italics his).

The most controversial passage in this connection is the one already noted, I Enoch 90.31, dating from the second century BC. It is true that Elijah is depicted there as one who comes down from heaven in readiness for the final judgment, but he is no more than a witness of the events that follow and does not play an active part in them. Dunn suggests that what we have here is to be understood simply as 'a visionary scene-changing, along the lines of, for example, Ezek. 3.12–15 and I Enoch 17–36' (ibid, p. 93) and not a picture of a deliverer from heaven. The other relevant passages in the pseudepigrapha come from the writings of the late first century AD or early second century AD. In Pseudo-Philo, for example, (late first century AD) the ascension of Phinehas (Numbers 25) is described in terms of the ascension of Elijah: he is lifted up into heaven and will remain there, says the Lord, 'and will not come down to mankind until the time arrives and you (will) be tested in that time . . . and you will be there until I remember the world' (Biblical Antiquities 48.1). Around the same time the same

125

notion of a heavenly ascent 'until the times are ended' is expressed by the writer of IV Ezra (14.9) and also in II Baruch where Baruch is to be 'preserved until the end of times' (13.3, etc.). The conclusion reached by Dunn seems justified: 'Such indications as there are point more to the decades following AD 70 as the period when such Jewish (and Jewish-Christian) speculation regarding Elijah and Enoch (and others) began to blossom' (ibid, p. 95).

(b) 'A prophet like Moses'

The other expectation, which finds expression *inter alia* in the Qumran texts and in the New Testament, refers to an eschatological prophet 'like Moses' whose word would herald the coming of the kingdom. The source of this expectation, as already noted, is to be found in Deuteronomy 18.18: 'I will raise up for them a prophet like you (Moses) from among their brethren; and I will put my words in his mouth, and he shall speak to them all that I command him.'

Such a hope was obviously alive among the covenanters of Qumran, as indicated, for example, in the Rule of the Community. There it is stated that the members of the Community will continue to live according to the original discipline 'until there shall come a prophet and the Messiahs of Aaron and Israel' (1QS ix.11). The same three figures are mentioned again in the Testimonies Scroll (4Q Testimonia) where the 'prophet' who is mentioned is identified with the prophet of whom Moses spoke. As a Teacher of the Law he is distinguished, in the context of these documents, from the other two messianic figures and it is possible that, in the minds of the members of the Community, he is to be identified with the Teacher of Righteousness who would 'rise in the latter days'. Be that as it may, it would appear certain that they expected a prophet like Moses at the end-time who would make clear to them the words of God.

Indications that such a belief was held in at least certain other circles within Judaism (and among the Samaritans) in the first part of the first century AD are to be found in the Gospels and in particular in the Fourth Gospel. When John the Baptist, for example, is asked, 'Are you the prophet?', he is in no doubt who is meant and he replies 'No' (John 1.21). Later on when Jesus had fed the multitude, the people likened this miracle to the miracle of the manna in the time of Moses and exclaimed, 'This indeed is the prophet who is to come into the world!' (6.14); and later still, when he offered them 'living water' to drink, they recognized the miracle of water from the rock and declared,

'This is really the prophet' (7.40). In the same Gospel the title is applied twice over to Jesus (6.14; 7.40), and in the Acts of the Apostles it identifies him as the suffering Messiah and exalted Lord (3.22; 7.37).

It would appear, however, that this identification of Jesus with the eschatological prophet did not prevail for any length of time and that in contemporary Jewish thought the idea of Moses the Deliverer, as a proto-type of the Saviour-Messiah, did not continue beyond the troubled years leading up to the fall of Jerusalem in AD 70. The reason for this may have been the rise in Palestine of men claiming to be the prophet promised of old and purporting to perform miracles like those of Moses in the wilderness. One of these was Theudas (Acts 5.36) who, according to Josephus, claimed that he would part the waters of the river Jordan as Moses had parted the waters of the Red Sea (*Ant.* XX.97). Another was 'the Egyptian' who stirred up revolt among the people and led them out into the wilderness pretending that they would behold wonders and signs (*Ant.* XX.167f.; Acts 21.38). It is not surprising that such pseudo-prophets for a while gained a measure of popular support; but in the words of Geza Vermes, 'As the promises remained unfulfilled and the miracles failed to materialize . . . the term "prophet" applied to an individual between the years AD 50 and 70 not surprisingly acquired distinctly pejorative overtones . . . It was no doubt for this reason also, and not merely because of any dogmatic inadequacy, that the title ceased altogether to be applied to Jesus: which is curious in view of the fact that it seems to have been the description he himself preferred' (*Jesus the Jew*, 1973, p. 99).

For Further Reading

Bartlett, John R. *Jews in the Hellenistic World*, CUP 1985

Charles, R. H. (ed), *The Apocrypha and Pseudepigrapha of the Old Testament*, 2 vols, OUP 1913

Charlesworth, J. H. (ed), *The Old Testament Pseudepigrapha*, 2 vols, Darton, Longman and Todd and Doubleday 1983 and 1985

Charlesworth, J. H. (ed), *The Pseudepigrapha and Modern Research with Supplement* (SBL Septuagint and Cognate Studies), Scholars Press 1981

Charlesworth, J. H., *The Old Testament Pseudepigrapha and the New Testament*, CUP 1985

Dunn, J. D. G., *Christology in the Making*, SCM Press and Westminster Press 1980

Ginzberg, Louis, *The Legends of the Jews*, Philadelphia 1909

Hengel, Martin, *Judaism and Hellenism*, 2 vols, SCM Press and Fortress Press 1974

Jonge, M. de (ed), *Outside the Old Testament*, CUP 1985

Kittel, G. and Friedrich, G. (eds), *Theological Dictionary of the New Testament*, E. T. Eerdmans, Grand Rapids 1964–74

Leaney, A. R. C., *The Jewish and Christian World, 200 BC to AD 200*, CUP 1984

Metzger, Bruce M., *An Introduction to the Apocrypha*, OUP 1957

Nickelsberg, George W. E., *Jewish Literature Between the Bible* and *the Mishnah*, SCM Press and Fortress Press 1981

Rowland, Chrisopher, *The Open Heaven*, SPCK 1982

Russell, D. S., *Between the Testaments*, SCM Press and Fortress Press 1960

—*The Method and Message of Jewish Apoclyptic, 200 BC - AD 100*, SCM Press and Westminster Press 1964

—*From Early Judaism to Early Church*, SCM Press and Fortress Press 1986

Scharlemann, M. H., *Stephen, a Singular Saint*, Pontifical Biblical Institute 1968

Sparks, H. F. D. (ed), *The Apocryphal Old Testament*, Clarendon Press 1984

Stone, M. E. (ed), *Jewish Writings of the Second Temple Period* (Compendia Rerum Iudaicarum ad Novum Testamentum, vol. II.2), Assen-Philadelphia 1984

Vermes, Geza, *The Dead Sea Scrolls in English*, Penguin ²1975

—*The Dead Sea Scrolls: Qumran in Perspective*, SCM Press ²1982

Index of Texts

Index of Subjects

Aaron, 91, 117, 126
Abel, 16, 17, 24
  as judge, 2, 78
Abimelech, 116, 118
Abraham, 69, 70ff.
  a legendary hero, 70ff.
  a religious genius, 74f.
  and angels, 82ff.
  and astronomy, 3, 72
  and Job, 59, 63, 64
  and Law, 2f., 74
  and legend, 4
  as friend of God, 77
  as observer of stars, 3, 72
  as wise man, 73, 101
  as wonder-child, 4
  condemns astrology, 72
  death of, 70, 77f.
  faithfulness of, 75
  father to world, 80
  founder of culture, 73
  in Apoc. of Abr., 68, 75ff.
  in Artapanus, 72f.
  in IV Ezra, 75
  in Gen. Apocr., 7
  in Jubilees, 69f., 70ff., 73f., 77
  in Philo, 2f.
  in Pseudo-Eupolemus, 69
  in Pseudo-Philo, 70, 71
  in Test. of Abr., 70
  kept whole Torah, 74
  learned astrology, 72
  long life of, 75
  merit of, 4
  obedience of, 74
  opposes idolatry, 74
  piety of, 77
  prayers of, 77
  righteousness of, 74, 75, 77
  speaks Hebrew, 73
  taught agriculture, 71
  taught astrology, 72

  ten temptations of, 74
  wisdom of, 2f., 73
  without mercy, 77
  without sin, 77
Abraham, Apoc. of, 70, 74, 75ff.
  Test. of, 7, 22f., 70, 77f., 79
Adam (and Eve)
  and Abel, 78
  and evil heart, 20
  and nudity, 104
  and resurrection, 17, 23
  and worship of Satan, 21
  androgynous beings, 18
  as angel, 18, 19, 23
  as fallen man, 19ff.
  as first patriarch, 13, 19
  as respresentative man, 19
  as 'second angel', 22
  as white bull, 23
  death of, 16
  deification of, 19, 23
  fall of, 16ff., 76
  glory of, 23
  in I Enoch, 23
  in II Enoch, 23
  in Genesis, 13f.
  in image of God, 13, 23
  in image of new man, 23
  in Life of Adam and Eve, 15ff.
  in pseudepigrapha, 14ff.
  in Test. of Abr., 22f.
  like eternal angels, 18
  literature, 17
  name of, 22
  on throne, 17, 22
  sources for, 14ff.
  time of, 31
  tradition, 19
Adam, Apoc. of, 15, 17, 19
  Life of, and Eve, 7, 15ff., 19
  Test. of, 7, 15, 18f., 23
Agrippa, 118

135

137

Index of Modern Scholars